CLIMBING
THE
MOUNTAIN

*Discovering Your
Path to Holiness*

By Anne, a lay apostle

Revised and Updated

Revised and Updated

CLIMBING
THE
MOUNTAIN

By Anne, a lay apostle

ISBN: 1-933684-46-1

Library of Congress Number: applied for

Publisher: Direction for Our Times
               9000 West 81st Street
               Justice, Illinois 60458

               708-496-9300
               www.directionforourtimes.com

Direction for Our Times is a 501(c)(3) tax-exempt organization.

Manufactured in the United States of America.

Graphic design and stained glass art by:
               Chris Deschaine
               www.braintrustdesign.com

How to Pray the Rosary information and the image of Our Lady Immaculate are used with permission. Copyright © Congregation of Marians of the Immaculate Conception, Stockbridge, MA 01263. www.marian.org.

All photos printed with permission.

Painting of *Jesus Christ the Returning King* by Janusz Antosz.

This book was written in
obedience to Jesus and Mary.
It is dedicated to all lay apostles
who seek to climb the mountain of holiness.

Direction for Our Times wishes to manifest its complete obedience and submission of mind and heart to the final and definitive judgment of the Magisterium of the Catholic Church and the local Ordinary regarding the supernatural character of the messages received by Anne, a lay apostle.

In this spirit, the messages of Anne, a lay apostle, have been submitted to her bishop, Most Reverend Leo O'Reilly, Bishop of Kilmore, Ireland, and to the Vatican Congregation for the Doctrine of the Faith for formal examination. In the meantime Bishop O'Reilly has given permission for their publication.

Table of Contents

Part One

The Rescue Mission

Welcome to the Lay Apostolate of Jesus Christ the Returning King. We serve Jesus by saying "yes" to Him each day in our duties. We serve Jesus by cooperating with Him in the process of personal holiness. Jesus never leaves us but sometimes we leave Him. We, as lay apostles, strive to remain with Jesus more completely in each moment so that He can use us to bring light to others.

"I am raising up a tidal wave of Christians to wash over the shore of badness that has taken control of this world, so lovingly created by My Father. This process will cleanse your world, making it safe once again for God's children. I am going to bring you knowledge, wisdom and love. I am going to introduce you to the divine to make your hearts burn like furnaces of divine love. You will be given the opportunity to work with Me. (Jesus, Volume One, p.1.)

The Rescue Mission

Jesus said that we live in an Age of Disobedience, which means that many souls are living in rebellion to God's will. He says that we are moving out of this time, toward an Age of Obedience, when most souls will live in unity with God's will. The time we are in now is a transition period.

A great renewal has begun, a rescue mission for souls. Jesus states that the Second Coming is a process, which will culminate in an event, grand and majestic. We are now in the beginning of the process. We do not know how long this period will last. We do not need to know.

Jesus is returning as King. In this initial phase of the process, He returns through each one of us. He is calling souls back to Himself, to serve as beloved apostles. He then floods each returned soul with light, a light which then overflows from the soul into the world. It is in this way that Jesus is restoring light to a world that has grown dark.

A great renewal has begun. Rejoice. Do not allow anyone to persuade you that we live in total darkness. There is darkness, yes, but this is not to be feared because it is quickly being dispelled. And while there may be darkness in the world, there is light and calm in the soul of each apostle. Rest in that light and calm when others attempt to draw you to pessimism, cynicism, or fear.

The shift toward obedience will require changes in our souls and in the way we live. Expect these changes. Rejoice in these changes. Jesus does not will fear for His apostles. Fear does not come from Him. Fear is a by-product of collaboration with the enemy. Our souls are destined for heaven and it is for this reason that Jesus has given us a glorious glimpse of our home there. Serve in joy and confidence as there is nothing to fear but a decision against God.

In this time, a powerful army of souls rises up in answer to the call of our Returning King. We agree to live in union with God's will, embarking on our personal path to holiness. Some of us have been apostles for many years and we have served ably in the world. Nothing has changed. We labor on.

Some of us are new arrivals in the heavenly army. Our commitment gives great joy to Jesus, Mary, and the saints. As each soul returns, a great cry of triumph erupts in heaven and our brothers and sisters there give praise to God. We grow daily in strength and number.

In order to organize and guide us, Jesus has called for the formation of a group He calls the Lay Apostles of Jesus Christ the Returning King. We serve where Christ has placed us, some in obscurity, others in the eyes of the world. We accept our crosses and carry them with the certainty that Jesus draws great graces from our cooperation and uses these graces for the conversion of sinners and the good of the kingdom. Indeed, the renewal is being fueled by the small daily sacrifice and service of each lay apostle.

Consider a mountain. On that mountain is a path that has been marked out carefully for each of us by Jesus. Jesus is at the top. The world is at the bottom.

If we get on that path and begin to climb, we will reach Jesus. We climb the mountain through our daily "yes" to Jesus. People say that they do not know the will of God, but God will not hide His will. We must spend time in silence and ask Jesus and He will tell us where our path lies on this mountain of holiness.

Most of us need look no further than to our vocations. Our path is usually marked out with the daily duties of these vocations and it is always best to begin at that point. In this time of transition, Jesus needs souls to find their path and start climbing. The higher we climb, the more grace and light Jesus flows through us into this world and the greater the number of souls saved. We praise God for the way He allows us to participate in this renewal.

Some speak of darkness and sin and the disobedience of many of our brothers and sisters. This darkness exists and we cannot ignore it. To do so would be to rest in denial. However, when souls talk more about these things than about the glory of Jesus Christ, it is clear that they are facing the wrong way on the mountain. Face up, dear friends!

Face Christ! Face heaven! If you do, you will be filled with heaven's joy and confidence.

If you face down toward the world you will become afraid. Also, when a soul faces the darkness he can risk becoming mesmerized by that darkness and drawn down into it. This is bad. Some souls are so busy studying the darkness that they ignore the light. Counsel souls to face Christ always and they will talk about joy and trust and heaven.

An important point to remember is that Jesus is far bigger than the Empire State Building, in terms of His power, His love, and His glory. The enemy is comparatively the size of an ant, a very small ant. The devil is like a little fire ant, it is true, and he stings, but ultimately he cannot topple the Empire State Building. Some souls, even some holy souls, are crowding around the little fire ant, marvelling at his miniscule power. They have forgotten that they do so in the massive shadow of the EMPIRE STATE BUILDING. We must all stop admiring the paltry power of the enemy of God and begin our climb with renewed determination, facing Jesus Christ and marvelling aloud at His power and majesty.

Mountain climbing can be difficult. I, Anne, your fellow apostle, have done my share of stumbling around. In obedience to Jesus, I have written Part Three: Climing the Mountain to chronicle some of my struggles and what I have learned from them. I ask that each reader understand that I am a learning climber myself, given to mistakes and short detours.

Contemplating the process of climbing our personal mountain of holiness should fill us with delight because once we reach the foot of the mountain and begin the ascent we are choosing the company of Jesus and all that surrounds

Him. There is no better place for us. Remember that no apostle climbs alone. We are together in the Spirit that unites us and each prayer sends assistance to others on the mountain. All eyes on Christ, dear friends. With Him, we cannot fail.

Part Two

Heaven

In late August of 2005, Jesus informed Anne that He would be allowing her to have experiences of heaven. Following is her record of these experiences.

August 28, 2005

Jesus said, *"You can see that I do not leave you, even for a moment. You should not fear this newest project because it will be similar to other experiences you have had. What will occur is this. I will take you mystically with Me for short periods of time. You will be aware in your senses, in as much as you will remain in your body. Your soul will accompany Me to heaven so that you can see what it is that I wish to show you. You will then record these experiences. My purpose in this is to reveal the truth to My apostles. Heaven is a truth. Souls serve Me on earth and they will then join Me in heaven. I am giving souls great courage through this grace. You need not worry over the publication of this work, Anne. That is My problem. I will reveal exactly how I wish these words to be disseminated. This project will be completed by mid-September. You will experience these visions with My constant companionship and you can talk to Me throughout and ask Me questions throughout, as you did today. Now, with the greatest trust and courage, record the small taste you were given today."*

I will try. Jesus drew me away from the crucifix, where I gazed, transfixed. He said, *"Leave My Passion for a moment and come with Me to heaven."* I did, and felt a sleepy kind of calm. I closed my eyes and rested in this calm and let Jesus' voice draw me away with Him. I was apprehensive in the beginning because Jesus had told me during Communion that this would occur. I began to see a vast area. There were distinct places but I got the strong and repetitive impression of no separations. I thought of a coliseum because these were places where great numbers gathered but there were no walls. It was like a middle place was raised. Jesus said:

"Souls who served together on earth, or who served in the same fashion, take the greatest pleasure in assembling for festivals or on feast days. There are many places for these gatherings. Let us join one."

We came closer and I could see a great number of souls sitting around a raised dais. I knew immediately that this was the gathering place of Franciscans. I thought I would see Saint Francis in the middle, speaking, because someone was there, but as we came closer it became clear that it was a woman. She was dressed like a queen except not showy. She wore a gown with terrific light movement. She was beautiful but I cannot describe her. She looked young and joyful and wore something on her head, a small crown that, while understated, was of the greatest quality. She was speaking to those gathered around. I said, "Jesus, who is it?"

"It is Clare," answered Our Lord.

She glanced at me and smiled and said, "*We have a visitor.*" I called out for Jesus and He began to speak again. He said,

"Look at this audience, Anne. They are all saints. Many served as Franciscans but there is

no separation in heaven so all are welcome. Many like the concepts being taught here so they bring others. There is constant joyous learning in heaven and such companionship provides the loveliest peace to others. Do not be afraid, Anne, because you are among friends. These souls know you and you will know them."

I was fearful again and I heard Saint Clare say, *"Let us take a moment and ask our Father to sustain little Anne so that she can persevere in His will."* I knew that this audience then grew silent and began to pray for me. I opened my spiritual eyes to look at the audience and saw two men in the front row. They had beards.

I said, "Lord, will souls have faces in heaven?"

Jesus was very patient and said, *"You will know each other, yes."*

That is what He said. We then backed away from this gathering place and Jesus brought me gently back to the room.

August 31, 2005

Jesus said, *"Record your experience. I will help you."*

Jesus drew me into Him and I experienced peace. He then said, *"What do you see, Anne? Look around you."* I saw trees. We were above an area of beautiful trees. As I looked down at them, Our Lord encouraged me to look more closely. I did and saw a stream cut into the ground. It was the most beautiful, clear water, moving steadily over rocks and moving downhill in a gradual way. I saw a woman on the other side of the stream from us. She was sitting on a rock, looking at the water and listening. I approached her, on Jesus' urging, and she gave me the most beautiful smile. She said, *"Listen, Anne. Listen to the sounds."* I did and the sound of the water was beautiful, like music. There was so much to it that it was like a symphony because there were so many different aspects of the sound. I had to settle in on small parts at a time. The music in a symphony blends together and you hear it as a whole. That stated, intellectually you understand that much has gone into the music's preparation and so many instruments come together and blend for the finished music. This stream was similar in that way.

Jesus said, *"You see that this saint is learning about Me from listening to the sounds of the stream. I created water, in its purity. She is contemplating My goodness in giving so many gifts to souls on earth. She is contemplating the depth of My wisdom as the Creator. She is learning about purity, about love, about the movement of the Spirit through all things created. Anne, this is how holy souls are on earth. When they contemplate the beauty of nature, they see Me. I am the Creator.*"

I thought of my spiritual director looking at the sunset as our airplane approached Chicago. He was awed by the majesty of it and said, "Imagine people trying to say God does not exist."

I asked Jesus if we would be eating in heaven. I realize how that sounds but I was curious. He said that we would not experience a compelling need to satisfy an urge. We would have different kinds of bodies in that we will not have to be slaves to our bodies as we are here. We will have feasting, but not in the same way. When I looked at the water, I wanted to drink it. He said that I will be able to taste things in heaven. When I was initially looking at the scene of the stream and the woman, He told me to listen.

He said, *"You have your senses, Anne. Listen to the beautiful sounds."*

I want to convey to souls how delighted Jesus was to be giving me this experience. He was so happy at my innocence in surveying the heavenly kingdom. He was so happy at my happiness. This is how Jesus will be for us all. He will introduce us to the heavenly kingdom personally. He is totally available to me during this time for any silly questions I have or any observations. This woman, Mary, an unknown saint, told me some personal things and asked me not to be afraid.

Jesus then drew me away and brought me further up the stream, and up, and up higher to the spot where the stream originated. It came out of a mountain and appeared quite unimpressive at its source. But from this small flow bubbling from the ground had come an elaborate run of water, growth, sound, beauty, and grace. The land near the stream, all down its length, was bordered by flowers and trees and all created things.

I asked Jesus if there were fish in the stream.

He said, *"Of course."*

I asked Him if we would eat the fish.

He said, *"No. You will not need to eat the fish."*

He was very patient and gentle. I want to say He was slightly amused at my questions but in the kindest way. I felt like a four year old who is completely safe and cherished and knows only total security. I love Him so much and everyone else will too.

He brought me up to very high ground and I could see mountains and valleys stretching as far as forever. There was no feeling of being hemmed in or crowded. I did not see any other souls but Mary. This indicates to me that there is total isolation if you desire it and complete companionship as well. I imagine I will go from one to the other as the alone time is spent with the availability of Jesus. I should remark that one of my impressions is that this heaven is very like all that is good on earth. We will be totally at home there. It is home. The nicest part of this all is Jesus. He bowls me over and I want to do anything for Him.

September 1, 2005

Jesus brought me with Him again. We moved over the area from yesterday and continued on past a range of mountains, the same ones I saw before. We moved swiftly and came down in what struck me as a city, but with no cars. I was aware of people, but not crowds. There was a square with something in the middle and beautiful pavement like cobblestones only bigger and intricately laid with perfection. There was a woman in the first floor window, holding a cloth in her hand. She was waiting for me. It was nicely warm or comfortable in temperature. There was no window, now that I think about it, just the opening in a beautiful stone building. There was no risk of anyone falling out, I guess, because it was the first floor and you would see at least glass on earth. I seem to get stuck on these details. I got an impression of who this was but said, "Jesus, who is this woman?"

He said, *"She is another Anne. You know her."*

I looked again and she was looking at me intently. This was my father's mother, my grandmother. I never knew her. She died before I was born. I pray for her every day though, and have had several strong experiences of her. She was a special woman, I know. She spoke to me and encouraged me. I was not listening very carefully and had looked away.

When I glanced back she met my gaze with the most piercing eyes and said, *"Don't be afraid. Your spiritual senses are not developed and that is why you are distracted. We are all here but we are also with you."*

Jesus said, *"Our little Anne is struggling today so we must all pray for her."* There were other people in the room with her and I wondered why they were together

19

because I knew them. They were all so happy. My grandmother gave the appearance of energy and business.

I said, "What are you doing in there?"

She replied, "*I am organizing. I like to organize things.*"

I said, "Are things disorganized in heaven?"

They all laughed. She said kindly, "*No. Things are beautifully organized in heaven. But sometimes I like to reorganize
them because it makes me happy. Anne, you will be very
happy here. You are like me and you like to be busy. I would
not be happy if I had nothing to do so I keep busy in doing
things that create order in the way I envision order. You are
creative. Your creativity will give you even greater joy here
than it does on earth.*"

We began to move away. Like yesterday, I did not feel any
sadness on leaving these souls because I know that I am not.
In a strange way, they are coming with me and I am remaining with them. I understand clearly that there is no separation between heaven and earth. I must remark that she was
with people I know, but people she could not have known on
earth. She, my grandmother, explained that they will be
together during periods by choice to greet me or meet me or
sustain me. The camaraderie between the souls in heaven
and the souls on earth cannot be stressed enough. We do not
have the divine vision yet, but they sure do and they use it to
help us in everything.

From here, Jesus took me away. I looked down and saw a
park. In the middle was a fountain. I had the impression of
a Japanese style of garden in one area, so beautiful and
orderly and gentle. Of course, I put my hand in the fountain
and became enthralled by the movement of the water. Water
seems special in heaven but I understand that it is my
enhanced perception that makes it special. There is the
beautiful noise of it, the movement, and today, the play of

light in the droplets enthralled me. Jesus allowed me to rest here. I am like the child who comes into a play room, filled with the most elaborate and magnificent toys, but who begins to play with the springy door stopper. The parent, in all frustration, tries to draw the toddler's attention to the magnificent toys but all the child wants to do is bounce the spring to hear the lovely ping noise. Only Jesus, unlike an earthly parent, understands that it is a lot to take in so He lets me rest by the fountain. He then shows me the scope of these gardens. This is a gardener's paradise and my sister will love it. Jesus shows me a beautiful bush. This has special meaning as I left some of these when we moved and I grieved for these silly bushes. No doubt that is why He has shown them to me. The gardens seem to go on forever. I am drawn away, back to the room.

"Anne, you are doing fine. It is not an easy thing to experience heaven while you remain on earth. At the same time, you can see that many of the things in heaven are similar to the things on earth in as much as these are created by Me to give joy to My children. You did not note the most important observation that you made to Me on your return to your chair. You said, 'Jesus, it is really all about love, isn't it?' And the answer is yes. It is all about love. My love for My children, My desire to please them and reward them, and the way My love flows through souls into each other. When you see love on earth, you know that I am present. Be at peace. This heaven has been created for all of God's children and all will be welcomed. The only souls who will not come to heaven are those who refuse My invitation. There is no need to worry over loved ones. They

are given the choice to make and most choose Me. But I need My beloved apostles to work hard during this time. Bring souls to Me while they are on earth. This is the best way. Bring My love to others and I can heal them and prepare them for heaven."

I want to add that yesterday, after I came back, I asked Jesus if we could swim in heaven.

He said, *"Of course you can swim."*

I would love to swim really far without a fear of drowning. I am not particularly buoyant here on earth and it takes great effort to stay afloat in the water. This has never stopped me from water sports, but it certainly has made them more challenging. So I will swim like a fish in heaven. Something else that I forgot to record is that Jesus told me on the first day that I would see family members in heaven, and people I know. I did not imagine that they would speak to me.

September 2, 2005

Today I walked with Jesus through a forest. The path beneath us was some kind of stone, smooth and worn and expensive looking. I can't describe it. Big warm stones, very smooth. There were trees around us and above them sunshine. The light was coming through the branches.

Jesus said, *"Look at the sunlight, Anne."*

I looked up, hesitating. I have a light sensitivity and would not look at any bright light without good sunglasses.

He said, *"It does not hurt your eyes. All of your physical infirmity is gone. Walk with Me in peace today and we will talk."*

I know I was surrounded by beauty but what interested me most was His presence and being with Him.

"Each soul on earth has a path that has been traced out for him. His culture, his parents, his placement in time, all of these things have been designed by Me. There are no separations in heaven so cultures and religions blend freely. You have seen the vastness of heaven, Anne, and yet you have seen only the smallest area. There is room for each soul and the reward for each soul has been prepared by Me."

I, of course, had the impression of an ant so I asked if there were animals.

"Yes. There are all things created here but there is no enmity between the creatures of God."

I said, "There is no hunting and no prey?"

He said, *"No. There is nothing like that."*

He said, *"Consider for a moment that you are finished on earth and that I have brought you here for eternity. How do you feel?"*

I considered that. I felt removed from earth but I did remember it and recalled so much pain. I said, "Lord, it was so hard. I would not want to do it again."

He replied, *"Look with Me, Anne. Look down at your suffering and see what I see. You can feel My love for you and even while you were on earth you felt My love. Look at one period of your suffering."*

I did and saw myself after a serious health problem. I had three children, and I was expecting a fourth. I was mostly on bed rest and could not manage the housework and the babies. It was a dreadfully difficult time. I winced, thinking of it and seeing myself in it, but I began to hear the prayers that were coming from me. This is what Our Lord was experiencing. I heard things like, "I offer this for you, Jesus. Help me, Jesus. I trust you, Jesus. Strengthen my husband, Lord. Stay with us, Jesus. Make me better, Lord. Bless these people who have to help us, Jesus." I saw our Rosaries being said with extended families. I heard so many prayers of suffering throughout the nights. I am writing this back on earth now and see what He is getting at.

During that period, I did not feel Christ as I do now. On the contrary, He seemed like He was gone if He had ever been there at all. This was a period of great suffering. The experience Jesus had in this period was the opposite of mine. He watched a soul carrying a great cross, who offered it all to Him. With this commitment, He built a fortress in my soul that He could occupy. This was one dark night for me but Jesus drew the greatest consolation from it. He blessed the souls who helped us. He blessed us. He blessed our children. From the heavenly perspective, great things were happening during this time. Standing next to Jesus looking at it, I was so grateful that I prayed and remembered Him in my suffering. The grace, while invisible and indiscernible to us, surrounded us. I can see that from here. I sure did not see it when I was in it, but I did believe it and I, in faith, knew that Jesus had not abandoned us. I knew Our Lady had not abandoned us. There was great peace in that house, I can see from here.

"You see the struggling, Anne. Talk about the struggles."

I was going to say that I could also see the enemy attempting to persuade us that we were being ill-used by heaven. We were good, so why did we have what appeared to be such bad luck and so many crosses? The enemy constantly tried to destroy my peace by showing me that others had it easy and were blessed with health and money and vacations. I see that I struggled continually to align my view to heaven's vision and made acts of love to Jesus in the face of these temptations toward bitterness. During this time I felt so sorry for my husband, that he was so heavily burdened. From here, I see that Jesus was making him a saint. This was part of my husband's process. My acceptance of the suffering obtained peace for him. But there was struggle.

"And from the struggle, Anne, came great holiness. Talk about My great peace in the face of your struggles."

Jesus is not shaken by the struggles. Even my bouts of anger at Him for my suffering do not upset Him. I bring my anger to Him and He takes it calmly, like the best life coach in the world. He understands that my view is necessarily limited and that my anger at Him is part of my process of acceptance of the cross. It occurs to me at this moment that

Jesus is trying to make us all saints. I am looking down at the process. I am not upset by my failures because I see them as my pain and my struggle. I am rather pleased that at least I gave Him some kind of return on His great love.

"That is it, Anne. It is this I want others to see. They will not avoid the cross on earth. If they accept the crosses in their lives, I can make them saints. Holiness is a process and suffering is part of that process. It is all about service to heaven, in suffering or in an absence of suffering. Talk about My acceptance."

If a soul walked away with one thing from this, I, Anne, would like it to be peace. Jesus loves us each. I feel total acceptance from Him. He is calm and kind. The word tolerant could be defined as "Jesus Christ." He is all Love. I feel that I will view things differently from this experience. That does not mean I will be casual about my service to Him because He is easygoing. It means I will walk with yet a deeper awareness of His involvement in each moment of my day. He is my Friend. He is your Friend. Each sigh, each prayer sent up in darkness with almost no hope, is heard by Him and He is interacting constantly in each moment of your day to give you exactly what you need to continue in spiritual growth. It will end, this life, and you will be so glad you gave Him each bit of fidelity and love. I see that my prayers were that much more powerful because of the darkness from which they burst from me. Praise God. We should strive for great acceptance in all because it is all from His hand and He never averts His gaze from us.

September 5, 2005

Jesus said, *"Record what you saw and heard, Anne. Do not be afraid. Simply speak the truth, as you know it, and I will help you."*

Our Lord took me back through the Valley of Solitude, where I initially met Mary, an unknown saint. He brought me up to the mountain range that borders this vast area and told me to look. I did, and became aware of many souls, sitting alone. From my vantage point, initially what I noted were the beautiful trees and growth, the slopes of the land, the rivers and streams. It was only after He called my attention to these individuals that I became aware of them. They seem to take up no space at all. I asked, "Is this called the Valley of Solitude?" I was already wondering how I would convey this to others.

He said, *"It is a valley of solitude. But it is only one of many. These are places where souls come to converse with Me in privacy and silence. They learn about Me and come to know Me better. As you know, there is no separation from Me here. But in these areas souls enjoy complete solitude, within which they can absorb more, and then more again."*

I understood and we moved on. Jesus brought me on past the city where I had stopped and spoken. I asked Him how souls moved here.

"Souls move at will," He replied.

Well, it certainly seems that way to me as my soul moves freely. I think we must move at His will because when He starts to move I move with Him. I guess that is obvious, given that we are in heaven and it is all His perfect will. We stopped at another building.

I was having trouble and He said, *"Anne, you are a child of God. You have every right to be here. Look, Anne. Look inside. What do you see?"*

Well, I saw a table, a beautiful table in a room that seemed to be a kitchen, except I did not see a stove. The table was wood and I was aware that there were men sitting around it. I did not look at them, as I could not bring myself to do so. Jesus told me to listen to them and I did. They were discussing events in the world. They were strategizing, it seemed to me. The theme or the general challenge being discussed was how they were going to bring the greatest number of souls to safety. I want to say that the threat to souls is from the evil in the world, not God's purifying events.

One man addressed me directly and welcomed me. He spoke and I knew him to have spoken to me before. He was Saint John of the Cross. He talked about the times. He told me that they were all there to help and that I was one part of a team. He directed me to the man at the head of the table. He told me that this was Saint Peter.

Saint Peter began to speak and I listened carefully. I was very aware that they did not budge when Christ entered.

Jesus said, *"Remember that I told you that there are no separations here. They are always united to Me so My entering the room does not startle them. You are the visitor, little Anne, and you can see that you are most welcome in this room."*

I asked Saint Peter if these times were darker than the times in which he lived. He said this:

"In my time men worshipped false gods. There was self-will, of course, and sin. The difference between my time and your time, though, is the level of arrogance. Man thinks he is a god. Man is filled with arrogance. The great learning and knowledge is generally not being used to further each other, but to advance self. This is not the way Our Lord intended man to live. Changes are coming, Anne, which is why you are here."

I asked him how I was supposed to speak to souls who were not Catholic. I get challenged to speak in a general Christian way, in order to touch more souls. Peter was very clear to me.

"You are a Catholic, Anne. You speak as a Catholic and souls will be drawn to Christ. You must preach what you are and what Christ has made you. The Catholic Church holds the deposit of our faith on earth, the truths. You must defend this. Souls who hear you will recognize the truth and they will recognize Christ. Fear no man. We are always close to God's apostles on earth and we will help each soul to represent Him. The renewal has begun. All must work."

I listened, aware that I was like the smallest child in this room, like a four year old in a room full of adults. I was comfortable with my smallness. Indeed, I felt safe in my humility because these men were also humble. That stated, they were making plans that would impact millions of God's children. Jesus trusted these men implicitly and relied on them to influence us and to support us. It appears that Jesus has no need to micromanage. He loves. Men and women work.

Saint Peter directed my attention to the other end of the table and it was John the Apostle. I rested in his great love and innocence, just staring at him. He then directed me to Saint Barnabas, who sat across from Saint John of the Cross. My impression of Barnabas was that he was the most agreeable and kind man.

The table was the most solid, durable piece of furniture I have ever seen. It was as smooth as glass, timeless in its strength and quality. Yet it was as simple a thing as I have ever encountered. I did not even notice the chairs or anything else. I kept my comfort by concentrating on the table. Peter continued to speak and told me to come to that room whenever I needed advice on the mission or advice for the apostles who were working on special projects for the mission.

He said, *"You are welcome here, Anne. We will direct you. When you are at a loss for words, come to John."*

He indicated Saint John of the Cross, of whom I know nothing. I was fearful at a speaking event once and Jesus told me that He was bringing me Saint John of the Cross, who would speak through me. This worked well as I was never at a loss for words.

"We will help you in everything," Saint Peter continued. *"You must be calm and work steadily, remaining in obedience. It will all work out."*

Jesus drew me away. I was left back in my room.

September 5, 2005

Blessed Mother

"Simply write what you saw and heard, Anne. I will help you."

Our Lady came and asked me if I would like to go with her. I was upset because of something that occurred right before and I asked for Jesus.

She said, *"I will take you to Jesus."*

She did but Jesus did not move to accompany us. He smiled and I felt more comfortable. Our Lady brought me through the places I had seen before. She stopped at the house in which the men sit around a wood table. I looked at their faces and they were filled with compassion.

She said, *"Many spoke badly about these people also, Anne. They understand. You will find great understanding in this room."*

We moved on and went to a place that was filled with flowers. There were groves and groves of flowers, all different kinds. We began to walk through the fields and Our Lady spoke.

"I am sorry that this hurts you, Anne. It is for this reason that I brought you here today. I knew you would be happy here. These gardens are filled with souls who were devoted to me during their time on earth. Each year, on the Feast of the Assumption, there is a festival and that is one of the occasions when all

of these flowers are arranged for a feast. I promised you I would bring you here and I always keep my promises."

It was at least a year ago that Our Lady asked me if I would like her to show me where they grew flowers for the Feast of the Assumption.

I saw white roses, peonies, lilacs in the distance, all kinds of delicate white flowers, some like baby's breath, some like little blue bells. The groves or gardens stretched as far as I could see and she smiled at me.

"Jesus is very generous to me, Anne. He is generous to all souls, of course, but He grants me great favors for my children."

I had the impression of souls around me, people, tending to bushes and beds. My heart was heavy and I had difficulty experiencing the joy. It would come to me in waves of happiness, to be with her, and walking with her, but then I would remember this hurtful thing.

"Anne, there will be those who seek to hurt you. Look at how they treat me."

Well, then I began to cry, right there on the path. The thought that anyone would hurt her just undid me. She started to speak. She consoled me so tenderly that I felt happy and joyful. My peace was restored and I was able to enjoy the gardens again. Our Lady began to speak.

"It is not possible for heaven to insulate apostles from all hurt, nor would we wish to. Anne, you have

seen heaven. You have experienced the peace and the love, the quiet contentment, the laughter and the happiness. Heaven is the home that each of our little children longs for. There is no substitute that will grant the security offered by the family of God. Dear apostles, if you are misunderstood on earth, rejoice. You will be understood in heaven. If you are hurt because of your work for Jesus on earth, rejoice, because in heaven you will be healed and ministered to with the greatest love. Anne, did you see one soul here who was grieving? Have you experienced anyone in pain or distress? This humble little work is about heaven, the destination of all just souls. Dearest little children, I beg you to treat each other with the love and respect that you will experience in the next life. Begin living like these saints while you are on earth and you will be brought directly here when it is time. You will not be sad that you offered Jesus your suffering. You will be grateful."

I am hesitant to describe how it felt to be consoled by Our Lady. I will not do it justice. She is the most merciful, and yet the most powerful woman I have ever met. You see that I fall miles short. Let me try again, calling on all of the saints. I would suffer for this mother. And I would do what I could to further her cause. Her cause is the cause of Christ, of course. To put it bluntly, I get the feeling there is a hard way and then there is Our Lady's way. She is the cushion that softens the fall. She is the one who walks you past your mistakes quickly, lest they discourage you. Our Lady will not fail us. She is too tender-hearted. I will be more devoted to her after this because of her kindness and understanding.

Again, I have to remark that being in heaven makes me feel like a four year old. They say that you have to be like a child to get into heaven. I believe it. There are no pompous or arrogant souls. No smugness or self-satisfied ones. The souls in heaven are filled with wisdom and kindness. And we are all going to heaven.[1] God is good.

---

1. What Anne means is that any soul who loves God will be welcomed in heaven. Clearly, if a soul rejects Christ he will not choose heaven.

September 6, 2005

Today Our Lord brought me with Him again. Through the valley and over the mountain ridge and into the city. I saw the same flowers that both border the paths and flow down through the middle. There are no cars. I guess that is obvious but I noted it today especially because there are buildings and they are separated by roads or pathways.

Before this, as we were moving through the valley, Our Lord asked me to stop and listen carefully. I did and heard crickets singing. Everything here seems to be consoling to me. I recently told a friend how badly I missed the sound of crickets singing. Well, I heard them in heaven so I will not spend any more time being sad about being away from this lovely noise.

I was brought to yet another building, through the open doorway and into a room in the front of the house. There were women gathered. I knew on the way that we were making our way to St. Anne, the mother of Mary, and Our Lord's grandmother. I did not have the impression of an elderly woman. She was beautiful. I did not look closely at the other women because I had difficulty. St. Anne began to speak. She welcomed me and offered me some advice. She then spoke about friendships in heaven.

"We are loyal to each other here, and take the greatest interest in the intentions of our friends. I tell you this so that souls on earth will understand how we conduct ourselves in heaven. If I receive prayers from a soul on earth who is asking for help with one who has a drinking problem, I will call on some of my friends here. I call on the friends who have the

most experience in those situations. We will sometimes gather to pray for an intention. With regard to the apostolate Our Lord has begun through you, it is good for all to know that we pray constantly for those who have answered 'yes.' When a lay apostle is embarking on a heavenly mission or project, he should call on us in a particular way. We have surrounded this mission with assistance and accompany each apostle on each errand."

I asked her if men and women mixed in heaven. There seems to be women with women and men with men. Nobody laughed today but today is a serious day.

"Yes, Anne. Men and women mix freely. Think of the group gathered with Clare. Think of the audience. There were men and women there together. We are just gathering with these friends at this moment. You have many women friends on earth and there are times when you find the company of women pleasing. There are other times when you prefer the company of men or like to be in a mixed gathering. It is the very same here. The only difference is that we seek only God's will. That is what we want. We want to help Jesus to further the kingdom on earth so that souls can be brought to safety. Anne, many are at risk at this time. And it is for this reason that God is sending so many graces.

"For now, think about your best earthly friendships. Those friendships most closely reflect the relationships here in heaven. I want to convey to souls that in heaven we work together and draw on the experiences of many to assist us in answering the prayers of God's earthly children. As you gather in prayer on earth, so we gather in prayer here in heaven. We pray with you and for you."

I glanced around and saw that there were five other women there. They were in various types of clothes and I thought that there were mixed periods in the room. I had the impression of different kinds of dress from different centuries, actually. Anyway, Jesus drew me away and we left. After this I rested with Jesus for a time, just thinking of it all and trying to take it in.

Jesus said, *"It is difficult to absorb when you are in pain, I know. Anne, your wounds will heal, as wounds do. They will disappear. But the graces obtained through your offering of your pain will not diminish. You will be in heaven and you will see the graces reflected in other souls who are here because of the generosity of those who suffered for them.*

"Be at peace, My beloved apostles. The pain you suffer on earth, be it physical or emotional, will be utilized. I use each little act of love, each little sacrifice. And when an apostle gives Me their day? Anne, I can do great things with such an offering. My beloved apostles who have been called from darkness during this time must serve in great courage and confidence. All that they suffer, all of their service, brings light into the world. I am pleased with such cooperation and prepare the reward for each apostle personally."

September 6, 2005

Jesus came for me and took me away with Him.

He said, *"Listen carefully to My voice and you will not be afraid. Let Me lead you and you will feel comfortable."*

What followed was the most lovely experience I have had yet. Jesus took me to the Valley of Solitude. We rested on the side of another stream and He told me to close my eyes. I heard birds and crickets. I heard an owl.

Jesus said, *"Do you like owls, Anne?"*

I said, "I guess they're okay, Lord. I don't know anything about owls. I don't like the thought of being in a dark forest at night and being afraid."

"Why would you be afraid?" He asked.

"Well, I don't like bugs and things or wild animals. Would I have to stay in the forest at night?"

Jesus then explained. *"There are souls who crave the soft darkness of the forest at night, Anne. They love the sounds, just as you love the sound of the crickets. So I provide these souls with exactly the peace they desire, in the darkness of the night forest. If you craved light, you would simply move to an area of the forest that was light. But there are many beautiful things about a heavenly forest at night."*

I thought about this and could see His point.

"Lord," I said, "that would be fine. I would like to be in the forest at night. But I do not want anything to crawl on me."

Jesus laughed loudly and so did I.

"I will not allow it, Anne. I promise."

I am afraid that I did not do justice to this night forest but I'm not sure that I can. It was the absence of light but not a total absence of light. There were soft shadows. The trees made the most beautiful noises as light breezes then heavier breezes blew through them. Sound is so sublime here. So beautiful. One could sit and listen for hours to the varying degrees of sound made by the winds blowing through the leaves. There were also many animal sounds, none of them ominous.

We moved on over the mountain ridge and through the city. Jesus said He wanted to take me to a special place. We rose up high, and higher up until the light began to change. It became a dark blue in some areas and darker again in others.

Jesus said, *"Look, Anne. What do you see?"*

I opened my eyes and I saw millions of stars against the night sky. We were up in them. Some were close and some were far. None were close enough to touch. It was beautiful and Jesus did not speak. Neither did I. I looked and looked, trying to get my fill. I craned my neck upwards and looked all around. It was wondrous. The most beautiful part, even of this, is the peace that flowed from Jesus into my soul. Jesus pointed down, slightly to the right. I saw the earth. It was beautiful.

"What do you see when you look at the earth, Lord?" I asked Him.

Jesus considered for a moment. *"I see hope, Anne. I see hope when I look at the world. I hear songs of praise and prayers of gratitude. My heart is moved to great mercy when I look at the world."*

I thought this was good, given all that has gone before and the need for this mission at all. This was a moment and trip for joy so I was not going to be the one to bring up the problems on the earth. Jesus was happy and so was I.

It was time to go and He told me that there was one small stop before we were to return. Back into the city, down a little side road, and into a door. A beautiful woman sat at the table, doing something with a bowl in front of her. It was Our Lady and I ran to her. She opened her arms and greeted me with such pleasure and love. Jesus, as always, was with us. But I sensed something different and it was this. Jesus was at home here, as He was at home on the earth. He began to tell me about this place. It was a humble kitchen with red flowers in a cup on the table. This was one of Our Lord's homes while He lived on earth. St. Joseph was there but I did not speak to him.

Jesus said, *"Many souls on earth long for a place that feels like their home. Anne, they will find that place in heaven. They will be with their loved ones and they will be at home, more so than they were ever at home on earth. I understand this longing as I experienced it Myself. This was My home and I felt happy in it. I have it here. Each soul will have a place here that is their home. Souls should understand that when they are forced to leave a home, it is only temporary. They will find it as soon as they arrive in heaven and it will be a joyful place, with none of the pain of their earthly home."*

There was terrific peace in this little kitchen and I did not want to leave. I simply did not want to go. Yet it was time. I asked Our Lady if I could come back to her here when I arrived in heaven and help her with whatever she was doing in the bowl.

"Of course you can, little Anne. You can come right to me here and I will wait for you."

Promise secured, we left and Jesus brought me back to the

room. I will be the only child in heaven, I'm afraid. Everyone else seems to be grown there, but I feel like the smallest of children.

Jesus said, *"Anne, you will not be the only child-like soul in heaven, I assure you. You are experiencing heavenly love and it creates an innocence that cannot be mimicked on earth. Have no fears. You are exactly as you should be."*

September 7, 2005

Today Jesus took me back to the Valley of Solitude. I rested there with Him and listened to the sound of the water. It was easier to hear this time. He explained to me that there were different areas in heaven and that the city I had visited was very close to the Godhead. The souls in that city had served Jesus with distinction. He said that all souls would have access to that city and would come there at some time. I think that the Valley of Solitude is a place where souls come before they enter the city, to prepare themselves perhaps.

We went into the city and entered a house, down a hallway and to the left. It was a large room and I was aware of approximately twenty-five people sitting in a circle. A woman spoke and Jesus asked me to listen to her. She talked about the situation on earth and urged the others toward the recommendation of a certain course of action. A man presented a different perspective and they discussed the topic back and forth. Jesus listened carefully to all, as did the others.

Jesus began to explain to me.

"These men and women are My closest advisors. They have great wisdom and concern themselves with the affairs of the Church on earth. They are aware of each detail as holiness ebbs and flows in the world. I listen carefully to their counsel because I trust them. They love each other so there is no aggression in their discussion. You can see that they treat each other with perfect respect. They are discussing the purification today, which is why I brought you to them. I want you to understand that each detail has been planned, not only

by Me, but also by souls who love as I love, and who seek only the advancement of My will. So you see, Anne, while it may look as though I have abandoned man, the truth is that I have planned each day down to the greatest detail. Do not view events with earthly eyes. View events with the goals of heaven in your mind and you will understand that all has been considered for the preservation of souls. The world is truly in the hands of heaven."

I understand that Jesus does not want me to fall into the trap of blaming Him for the difficulties in the world. I did have trouble last night when I viewed so much suffering. It is important to understand that God is in charge.

Later, Jesus brought me back to the same room. The man was now talking and Jesus asked me to listen, as what he was saying was important and part of the reason that Jesus had brought me here. The man spoke of the loss of heavenly influence on souls in their youth. He said that heaven should no longer allow children to be poisoned by the erroneous beliefs of their parents. He also cited situations in schools that drew children toward the enemy. The woman across from him nodded in agreement. She seemed to be quite an authority in the room. The discussion involved our children.

I said, "Jesus how will You fix this?"

"We will have to work through the parents, Anne," He replied. *"This is part of his argument for the course of action he favors."*

We left that area then and moved up into the dark blue of the sky, far up into the stars, where everything is far away and yet all seems close. It is a very big place, this universe.

September 7, 2005

Jesus brought me to the Valley of Solitude and we sat by the stream again. He talked about the mission and helped me to understand why He was giving this grace. He said that these glimpses into the heavenly kingdom are intended to inspire man to service and to help us to reject the fleeting material things that the world offers. We are to understand that what will endure will be our service, our love, and our devotion to our duties. He said that these glimpses would result in conversions because of the graces attached. He will communicate with souls through this work so that they will have a greater mystical capacity than before.

There is a lot of what I see that I cannot attach words to so I leave it with the peace that comes from Christ. How do you describe total security and love? I guess you can say that it is the complete absence of anxiety. That would be one way but only a small facet.

Jesus took me across the city and into the sky. Instead of going up into the heavenly universe, we crossed this sky, which was that glorious mix of blues and darkish colors, until we came to a different day. It was light then and we crossed another valley and entered a different city. This city was bustling. I had the impression of many souls.

Jesus reminded me to open my eyes and I locked onto the first person I saw, an Asian man. He had a ready smile as he prepared some kind of conveyance. I did not have the eyes or understanding to grasp what he was doing but he was a dignified man and I loved him immediately. Everyone in heaven is beautiful. This feeling of camaraderie is instant and complete. He stood in front of a building on a street where there were many buildings. Jesus told me that we were going in. As we stepped in the door I saw that it was kind of a church. There was an atmosphere of the greatest reverence. I looked at the audience and they were enraptured by what was occurring in the front of the church. Their faces were lit with joy and they all sang in sweet and soft voices. I wonder if they were Catholics as it's hard to get this kind of singing from Catholics on earth. Jesus said they were from different religions. They were certainly from different races. There was a complete mix of skin colors and bone structures. All were beautiful. I really do not know sometimes if I am seeing souls or faces. When I concentrate I do see faces. At any rate, all had a radiant look of love in their eyes.

I searched for the object of this love and saw Our Lady at the front of the church. They were singing to her.

I said, "Jesus, help me to understand what they are saying."

I could not get words, just harmonies. And the harmonies were glorious. I was then able to discern certain words, including the word Mother. These souls were learning about Mary. Again, I must note that nobody reacts when Jesus enters. He mystically never leaves them. I had the impression of Christmas here in this church. There was a sense of wonder and innocence that I associate with Christmas. The priest at the front of the church, if it was indeed a church, was leading the praise. I could not share in what they were witnessing and this saddened me. I wanted to see what they saw and experience what they were experiencing. But I am here on a guest pass so it is not time. Jesus conveys to me that I will do so in the future.

It seems that souls have limited experiences on earth. Some have never heard of Mary, as difficult as that is for me to imagine. These souls get to learn about her in heaven. I am filled with the depth of divine justice and benevolence.

Take a soul on earth who has not been exposed to any faith at all. He comes here to heaven and he is able to absorb the greatest mysteries of the Godhead and the kingdom of the divine. We must never pity a soul who dies as a child or dies without having any depth of faith or knowledge of faith. If the soul chooses Christ, that soul will experience it all and learn it all. My attempt here is pitiful, I know. I trust the Spirit to bridge the chasm between the reality and my attempt to represent it.

We leave. Jesus brings me across the street or road and we enter another church. This is a building dedicated to Saint John of the Cross. There are souls looking at various elements of his life and teaching. They are learning about concepts that they were not familiar with from their lives on earth. Jesus talks about learning and how it continues in heaven. These souls do not look bored. As in the last building, they have faces filled with wonder and awe. There are groups together, with one soul indicating various elements to others. There are souls on their own, gazing in silence at those displays that are not available to me. This John must be something. But Jesus indicates to me that in each life there are moments of great value and dedication or triumph over self. These moments are preserved. There is no sense of sin here at all. There is no sense of anything but joy. I cannot convey this and it makes me sad because I want to do it justice for souls on earth.

This area, while not crowded, is a lot busier than the city across the blue/black universe. There are the same flowers and trees and again, the beautiful sounds. Outside there is lovely light and the sound of breezes. Inside this building, where souls are studying Saint John's spiritual triumphs, there is a delicate chime sounding. It is not one note but a lovely quiet melody made up of the most exquisite notes. It provides a background of serenity and adds to the wonder. You could really come here just to listen to this music. I am made aware that this city is made up of countless buildings like this. Jesus talks to me at length about learning and how it continues in heaven, giving great joy to souls.

We step out into the light. I see souls again together and alone, all looking peaceful and some chatting.

I am back to my room at home with the words wonder and awe on my lips.

September 8, 2005

Today Jesus brought me to sit with Him by the stream. We spoke for some time about my role in this mission. I have been struggling with some issues and Jesus explained how I am to conduct myself. I was able to ask Him many questions.

Afterwards we moved along the same course as yesterday, out of the valley, past the mountains, over the city and across the star-filled bluish sky. We entered the city where it is a new day and stopped again in front of the building that reminded me of Christmas. We entered.

Today it was vast. Souls filled this area and it seemed like the greatest cathedral. Our Lady was in the middle. Jesus instructed me to listen carefully and I did. A man was singing to her, a solo, and all souls listened and enjoyed the beauty of this loving voice that sang as a gift to Our Lady. This man was not a famous singer on earth. He was an unknown saint, as are most saints. The voice carried through the cathedral with absolutely no unnatural vehicle. There were no microphones. I listened and was drawn into the beauty of his voice, the love in his song. I was keenly aware that all of the souls present were enjoying this voice in the same way. It was a gift to Our Lady but also a gift to us all.

After he finished his song Our Lady thanked him. I did not see him. Our Lady was different than everyone else in that her movements seemed natural to me. She was not ethereal. She seemed to move as I would expect a person to move. Is that saying that nobody else moves normally? I don't think so. I am just not aware of the way others move here, but I am aware that Mary moved naturally and I could see her arms moving. She held flowers in her hands.

She had a veil on. It was white. Over the veil was a crown. In the middle of the crown was an exquisite blue stone that represented her maternity. Many other stones surrounded that one. She is as pure and lovely as it is possible to be. Jesus told me to look at her carefully so that I could describe her. I could see that she was very happy. Jesus told me to look carefully at the scene.

Our Lady was surrounded by flowers. Each flower was an offering from one of the souls here to see her and to greet her on her birthday. I recognized some of the flower varieties and saw white roses. I also saw lilacs. This next point is important. There were many souls present. Countless. But each soul communed with Our Lady as though he or she were the only one there. So their time at this event or celebration was together with other souls, but also in separate unity to Mary. They could talk to her and converse with her as they wished.

She turned and spoke to me directly and the festivities carried on. So she was not ignoring anyone else when she spoke to me, but our conversation was distinct to us. I hope I am clear. She told me that souls come to her all through this special day. I asked her if she was given gifts because I did not see any presents. She said no, that each soul there was her gift and she considered every soul in heaven a gift to her because she considers each her child. Jesus has given her many graces for souls and when the soul is in heaven, Our Lady looks at the soul and sees the mercy and generosity of Jesus in them. That is her gift and it will endure forever.

She explained that one of the special things that occurred on this day was that she granted great favors to souls, favors she obtained from Jesus. She said that Jesus is very generous on these special days, her birthday and feast days. I was thinking that this is the day to ask for things and she read my thoughts.

"What does my little Anne want today?"

I thought fast because I realized I had a lot of people who would be grateful for a mention at this moment. I could not single anyone out. There were too many. So I asked her to grant the intentions of anyone who has ever asked me to pray for them. I held my breath, knowing this was big, but I have long since learned that when one is dealing with heaven it is best not to limit our requests.

She gave me the most beautiful, intimate smile, and all of the other festivities faded away. Her voice seemed to fill me and echo through me. **"I will give this to you, Anne. I will grant favors to all who seek your intercession, both now and in the future. This is a special day for me, both in heaven and on earth. Jesus will refuse me nothing."**

I have to make another point here. All of these souls are saints. They are the Church Triumphant. They are all there and they have all brought intentions. This is not a greedy thing. They lack nothing. They are in heaven. They are not asking for themselves. They are petitioning for souls on earth and attempting to impact what happens on earth. We have not been abandoned.

I think that too few are asking for graces in this time because there are enough graces for all good things. And yet we do not have all good things in the line of virtues and humanitarian relief. But we have a lot of good things in our world and we have the opportunity to obtain great changes in that heaven is prepared to give freely during this time of renewal. So we must begin asking. We should ask all the saints to intercede for us. Today I saw them doing it. They had all brought petitions regarding their loved ones as well as for heavenly projects on earth.

It was time to go and I leaned back into Jesus, who is

always behind me. Often during these experiences I call out to Him and His voice answers immediately. When I leaned back into Him He surrounded me and I felt so safe. Heaven is all wonderful. Our Lady is the joy of all joys. But I have to state, and she would want me to do this, that Jesus is everything. He is everything. Nobody reacts when He enters, I say again, because He never leaves. They must all experience Him as I do and maybe that is why they do not react. I know there is no separation. Jesus is in everything and surrounds everything. I can't say enough about how kind He is and how loving. I find I have to give a deep sigh and stop trying.

He led me gently back into myself.

September 8, 2005

In response to my question, Our Lord said, *"Write it exactly as you experienced it."*

Jesus brought me with Him, explaining that this would be a short experience. He asked me where I was, twice, I think to help me to be aware. I was over the valley that leads into the city. When we got there, we turned to the left, instead of going straight on, which would be toward the blue night sky with the stars. We traveled in that direction for a time and came to the end of the city. There was a divide of some sort that led to a structure that was huge. We entered and Jesus asked me what I saw, to prompt me to look.

I saw a lot of people gathered in a semi-circle. They were waiting to see God the Father. Jesus said it was important to understand that there is a distinction between Jesus and God the Father. Jesus reminded me that He had brought me to God the Father before. This is true. I had an experience of it many years ago. I was not as afraid after that because it was a beautiful experience.

Jesus brought me to Him and I felt His piercing gaze go through me. My first thought was that this was the One I pledged my allegiance to at the Consecration of the Mass for years. He had heard me for years. All of those prayers were in His eyes in some way. It's as if all of those prayers were with me at that moment. He had been listening. God is paying attention.

The second thought that went through my mind is that quite simply, this Man, this God, knows EVERYTHING. No point in trying to get out of anything here. God knows it all.

There is nothing hidden from His gaze. He was serious, in the extreme. I felt no fear, only love.

He said this: *"You are cherished. You know that I cherish you as My beloved servant. Anne, just as I cherish you, I cherish each soul. Work for souls. It is for this reason you have been called."*

He returned His attention to whatever He was doing when Jesus brought me to Him and I backed into the warmth of Christ. I was a little shaken and Jesus spoke to me quietly. After a time I came back to myself.

When I did, I asked, "Jesus, I understand you and God. What is the Spirit?"

He reminded me of the Valley of Solitude. During one of these experiences I saw a bird flying high, drifting in a stream of wind. The bird did not move its wings. It just remained still and the wind held it high above the forest. I don't know how long I stared at it but I could not take my eyes from it.

Jesus said, *"It is the Spirit that held the bird aloft, Anne. The Spirit is what connects all goodness. It is the Spirit that bound you to the Father. The Spirit moved through you, prompting you to pledge your allegiance to the Father, and the Spirit has sustained you since your Baptism. The Spirit supports all. Souls must ask for this Spirit and welcome Him."*

I'm thinking that it is the Spirit that seems to highlight one sentence in the Bible when you are reading and it seems to hit you hard or when it illuminates you completely.

I have also found that the wind blowing through leaves and moving the trees holds me spellbound. That must be the Spirit too. I am very aware of this Spirit in my days.

September 9, 2005

This morning Jesus gave me the opportunity to ask Him questions. I did this for a long time. This conversation took place in the Valley of Solitude, by the stream, as usual. I was able to listen and rest and this was pleasant. I closed my eyes at one point and listened at length to the sound of the leaves. The wind is alive here and as I felt it on my face I was drawn back to a time in my life when I had a similar experience. I had closed my eyes at that time also, and felt a soft breeze on my face. At the time, I knew it was a heavenly presence. This was well before my conversion. I was young and at a difficult place in my life. But I knew that the caress on my face was not from earth and I was comforted by it. This felt the same.

It is all love in heaven and even the breeze ministers to souls. Recently someone asked me what Jesus looked like. I was startled because I did not know. I don't think I really see Him. I was alert today, for this reason, and realized that I am not so much looking at Him as united to Him. Heaven is unity to Christ. He is with you completely and you do not want anything else.

After a time He drew me away. We went into the city and turned left toward God the Father. Instead of continuing on, we turned right shortly before we would get to that big structure. Jesus brought me to another large structure and I understood that we were visiting the Passion. I did not want to do this.

Jesus said, *"Unity is complete here, Anne. Souls often visit the times of My life on earth. They do this to enter into the mystery of what was accomplished by God during those years. Time is different here. You understand this. The life and accomplishments of each saint are commemorated. In the same way, My life and accomplishments are honored. A good friend seeks to understand the difficult times as well as the joyful times. My Passion is alive here so that souls can enter fully into the mystery of the Redemption. Remain with Me for this short time."*

I did. I saw Jesus in the Garden and I entered immediately into the suffering. I felt it as a dreadful anguish and revulsion. This went on later as Jesus was pushed and pulled, mocked, spit on. I saw Jesus being whipped. This is how I saw it. I had an awareness of Jesus during His Passion, from the Garden to His death. I am having the greatest difficulty because I truly do not want to revisit this. The awareness would pause on highlights, which were the scourging, the crowning, the horrific carrying of the cross, and the crucifixion. I had the most horrid view of His poor little legs, which trembled under the weight of His broken body. The only way to cope with these experiences is to focus in on small details and this is what I did. Hence the fixation on His poor little thighs and legs.

I cried out and said, "Jesus, is this happening now?"

His voice came within me. He said, *"No. I am here, Anne. I am not suffering in this way now. But My Passion is honored in heaven and souls come here to be with Me in a mystical way. It is important that souls know that the depth of My sacrifice can be understood in heaven. This is a part of union, Anne, and you will come to experience this more gradually."*

We left this area and I came back to myself, a little shaken.

Part of the reason this shook me up is this: In this heavenly experience, there is perfect clarity of the innocence and goodness of Jesus. He is the Lamb, the spotless One. He is all Love, all Goodness. And He is being tortured. I mean the nicest adult on earth at this time is still culpable for something, I would think. But not Jesus. He did nothing but serve. And this is where it took Him. It is a good example, indeed the perfect example, of love and service to both humanity and to heaven. This awareness makes it even more excruciating for me because I am not a resident of heaven. If I were, I would not feel shaken up. I would be gaining in understanding and knowledge. I would be entering the depths of His Passion and growing in wisdom of the sacrifice. This experience brought me clearly to the understanding that my work on earth is not finished. If it were, I would be at peace in His suffering. As it stands, I have my own suffering yet to complete. When I have, and when I am fully purified, I will be able to gaze upon this Passion in heaven and not be filled with remorse, but with love and gratitude.

September 9, 2005

We went through heaven via the same route. I felt joy and freedom. The greatest joy is asking Jesus questions. We turned right sooner than the Passion and I saw yet another vast structure. Jesus told me that this was the house of the Resurrection. He asked me to describe what I saw.

I saw millions of souls in rapture. They were riveted to the raised area in the front. I saw Jesus there. He looked similar to the Divine Mercy image only real. His hair was dark brown, it seemed to me. He was beautiful. He was love. All souls looked on Him and I understood that they had completed the study of the Passion. These souls were enraptured. There was another area and I asked Jesus what was there. He explained that His tomb was there. As I understand it, you can revisit the whole experience. In looking at these souls I was struck that they were in complete communion with Jesus. They were in Easter Sunday joy. It also ran through my head that some of them were there for millions of years. That was the longest time I could humanly attach to it. They were not bored. They were in ecstasy. The term millions of years means nothing, of course. It's just my way of saying a really long time.

Jesus said, *"Anne, this is important. These souls have entered into the mystery of the Resurrection. The greatest understanding of man on earth cannot compare to the smallest kernel of understanding in heaven. With understanding comes joy and wonder and reverence. It is for this reason souls gaze so long upon the Risen Christ. I make all of this available in heaven and souls come here often. Souls are welcome to rest in any of the heavenly mysteries. All is understood here. All is accepted. All is just. Souls feel only peace."*

Part Three

Climbing the Mountain

Love of Neighbor

Clearly, the love of Christ is meant to be shared. After the experience of heaven, I can see that the kingdom of God is made up of souls who love each other. If Christ is in each one of us, and this is of course what we believe as Christians, then we must venerate Christ in every soul. How do we do that?

We do that with respect and gentleness. Some might say, "Yes, this may be true but I see souls in error, in mortal sin, living far outside of the heavenly kingdom." Well, dear fellow apostles, this is when the call to treat them as Christ is at its most profound. If Christ has indeed been driven out of a soul, through serious sin and a spirit of rebellion in that sin, then the call to illustrate our unity with Christ is compelling. How does Christ treat that soul? How does Christ view that soul? I will tell you.

Christ does not glance at a soul and see the sin, although He is acutely aware of the sin. Christ glances at a soul and sees the wound that both caused the sin and was worsened by the sin. So in order for the kingdom to come, and it must and it will, we must treat each other as Christ would.

Sometimes a soul living outside of the kingdom is bitter. This bitterness is like a sore. When a soul in bitterness views Christ in us, it can be like salt in the wound or sore because our unity with Christ highlights his isolation from Him. This is good. The soul then comes closer to an understanding of what it lacks. Our experience of this may not be pleasant. It may be necessarily painful because in its pain his soul may strike out at us. This can be understood as an almost instinctual lashing out or crying out in the distress of his disconnectedness from Christ. We must accept these strikes as beneficial penance and part of standing with Christ as a companion on the Way of the Cross.

To clarify, I am driving in traffic and I make a mistake perhaps, or commit a deed that inconveniences someone else. I give the other driver an apologetic wave. He responds by swearing at me, shouting and threatening. This is shocking for a holy soul.

We must offer this to Jesus. We must bring that soul to Jesus in prayer and petition. Our prayer will obtain critical graces for that soul. We must look at this person and see the wound, the sore.

To be more specific to the call to bring Jesus Christ to souls directly, consider a soul who is estranged from the kingdom. Perhaps it is a family member or neighbor. It is possible that he may be unkind to us because our holiness is an irritant to him and to his wound. Is it then acceptable to be unkind in return? No, this is not acceptable for an apostle of Jesus Christ who seeks to bring His love to them. Remember that it was AFTER the Crucifixion that the Centurion said, "Truly, this was the Son of God." That soul only saw Christ through the manner in which Jesus accepted suffering from the offender's hands. Note this parallel.

A soul may be tormenting us, but for this soul to experience Christ, we must accept it as Christ would. This should be in flashing red lights.

We may be praying for this soul and beseeching heaven for the conversion of this soul. So we must not complain at a little suffering for this soul, particularly if it comes from the hand of that same soul.

It helps to examine our motives. Do we want this soul to be saved for the sake of the soul and for the consolation and glory of Jesus Christ? Or do we want this soul to be saved so that the soul will treat us better and make our life easier? I think perhaps it can be a bit of both and this is acceptable. But as we begin to lean more to the benefit of both the soul and the kingdom, we will become more willing to accept the occasional bad treatment for the purpose of the greater good, which is the salvation of the soul and the consolation of Christ, as well as for the benefit of the kingdom.

We must bring souls to Jesus, but we must not take Jesus and bash souls about the head with Him. We must bring Jesus in the spirit of love, not condemnation. The message is that Jesus loves the soul, not that Jesus disagrees with the way the soul is living his life. Is it true that Jesus disagrees with the way some live their lives? Yes. Certainly Jesus was not always pleased with the manner in which I conducted myself. But it is best to let Jesus convey this to the soul. Jesus judges. Apostles are not called to be judges but delivery people. If we deliver Jesus to souls He Himself will correct them, tutor them, and illuminate their path on the mountain. You might say that the most profound thing we do for a soul is to show him the mountain.

As in everything, the most effective way to teach something is to set an example by doing it so that others can emulate us after seeing how a thing is done. This brings us to the most important concept of all concepts.

We must always be ascending. What is the best way to love my neighbor? I love my neighbor best by climbing my mountain of personal holiness. It is not helpful for me to spend my time telling others to climb. It is helpful if I myself climb, thereby setting an example for others to follow.

Love of neighbor is love of Christ and love of Christ involves love of duty, service, and vocation because it is through these things that we achieve a perfected love of Christ.

We must view each other as souls on the mountain path. We must be cheerfully friendly to others, particularly those who are walking with us for a time. We never know when a companion will be called home. We must treat each other with this in mind. A soul accompanying us may have only this day to continue his ascent.

We should be gentle and loving with each other, always tolerant that no two servants are called to serve in exactly the same way. Each has separate gifts, so we must never think it is beneficial to compare ourselves with anyone. We may find temporary satisfaction in this, considering that we are holier, but when measured against the divine yardstick, which always considers what we have been given in the line of graces and gifts, our advantage may quickly diminish and disappear.

We must compare ourselves to Jesus in love of neighbor. Scripture gives us plenty of examples of the selflessness with which Jesus served His brothers and sisters.

He was a dutiful Son to His mother and father. He was a good friend to His apostles. Jesus was kind to strangers and those ill and less fortunate. He was patient in the extreme with the flaws of others. He saw each soul as a soul who was somewhere on the mountain and He viewed them with the patience of a teacher, who knows that the total cannot be achieved without walking through the equation. Jesus gave others the room to grow in the light of His love. Are we doing that for others?

Or do we constantly point out the deficits in the holiness of our companions?

Souls loved Jesus and sought out His companionship. They sought His love and tolerance, His acceptance and steadiness. This is our call to those around us. We must always rejoice in the holiness of our companions. Rejoice in each bit of progress or any bit of hope for progress. This will give us joy and we will not spend all of our time lamenting the failures of those around us, which is really our own failure.

It is good to realize, in the area of patience, that many souls remain outside of the kingdom for a long period. Be hopeful and patient when you pray for the conversion of a soul. Remember that when he returns, he can make the greatest strides in holiness in a short period of time. This is yet another reason to be filled with joy. We should not look at a soul who comes to the Lord and see the years of non-service. We must never do this, for ourselves or another. Instead, we must look at the joy of the return.

The father in the Prodigal Son story did not reproach his son. He did not sit down with him and grieve the lost years. He went straight to the celebration and rejoiced in the future service of the returned boy. This is the way our God reacts to returning children. He sees what the child of heaven is now capable of giving to the kingdom. He sees the potential and the lovely swell of the family, given the return of a loved one. Remember that the laborers were all given the same wage, regardless of when they joined the work. This is an example of a good and gracious God, not an unjust God. We can use this to pull others in. Each servant is as necessary as the next.

Remember that there is little merit in loving those who love us, but great merit in loving those who are a cross to us.

September 22, 2005

It is through our closest relationships that we make the most dedicated progress up the mountain because those closest to us see our flaws clearly. We should pray for an increased awareness of our performance in the duty of the relationships closest to us.

It is within the structure of the family that many souls find great holiness. This is why Jesus is so determined to protect the family and this is also why the enemy is so anxious to destroy this heavenly structure. Family members see our flaws, yes, and often it is only a family member who has the courage to illuminate this flaw for us. We must not retaliate in anger if a loved one encourages us to alter our behavior. We should instead be open to the possibility that he may have a perspective that will benefit us. An arrogant soul cannot tolerate any criticism or direction. He will revolt and lash out at the one who dares press against his shell of self-satisfaction. We discussed the Way of the Cross and the pain that comes with it. Be at peace in this.

Before we begin to instruct someone or gently correct a soul, we must pray. We should spend time in silence and ask Jesus if it is He who is prompting us to assist a soul in this way. We should then proceed in all humility, certain that despite our closeness to Christ, we have a pack full of our own flaws to work upon. Our spirit should be one of kindness and tolerance. What would Jesus say to this soul? How would Jesus proceed?

In my experience of Jesus, He uses few words. His reprimands or corrections are short and powerful, often only one sentence, which He repeats. He tells the truth and there is no self-interest in His workings. Always think of the good of the soul.

It is important to comment now on the souls who take advantage of the family structure to exhibit a pattern of selfish and unkind behavior. This is not Christian. This is answerable in heaven. If heaven is everywhere, and it is, and Jesus is always present, and He is, there is nothing that will be hidden. Each interaction with each family member is conducted in the full presence of Jesus Christ and all of heaven. So if we confine ugly and unkind behavior to those closest to us, assuming we will not be identified because of their silence and fear, we can be assured that there will come a day when our motives will be laid bare before us and we will answer for each act. If we are not at peace with this thought, we should amend our behavior immediately.

Perhaps we are living with a soul such as this. We are praying for him, we are asking for help from heaven, but we are fearful of his wrath should we attempt to correct him. In this case we should seek counsel from Jesus and ask that He give us the words and the direction. He will not fail us. Truly, my friends, it is not good for a person to get away with constant bad behavior as it confirms his path. In cases where we are fearful of our family members, we must consider seeking outside help. We should confide in someone, perhaps a trusted priest who can advise us objectively.

Jesus understands that we are doing our best. We must understand that we are part of a heavenly team who shares our goals for all our loved ones. Remember that there are apostles the world over praying for our safety and peace.

The family is a microcosm of the heavenly kingdom. Each family is a little kingdom of God. This proceeds out in concentric circles, bigger and bigger. But it begins first with one soul united to Christ, then spreads into the immediate family, and then out and so on. We must do the work first in our own little soul, united to Jesus; then in our own little family; then out and out and out again, into the world; and eventually at one with the whole kingdom of God. The importance of the work done within the family cannot be stressed enough. It is here we learn how to be a Christian. It is here we learn how NOT to be a Christian. It is within the family that we learn about compassion and sacrifice and tolerance and forgiveness. Progress is made in quietness and the progress of one soul impacts the entire family. We must be confident that our holiness will spread out into our families. It cannot help but do so. If we never say a word about Jesus Christ, but begin to live His message, we will benefit our families in ways we cannot understand. The holiness of one soul creates a receptacle of grace for all. Again I stress, even if we are estranged from all of our family, but we decide to follow Christ in isolation from them, we will draw blessings down upon them all. It cannot help but be so, given Christ's goodness and desire to reach each of His children. We must be at peace in everything, dear apostles. There is no reason for anything but peace.

Sometimes in describing a thing it is good to say what it is not, so that souls can move closer to truth by abandoning what is false.

Love of neighbor is not judgmental. It is not unkind, ever. It is rather gentle and patient with the frailty of the soul, whether the soul is on the path or drifting in the world. Love of neighbor assumes the presence of the loving God in the soul of each person and treats each person accordingly. How do I treat Jesus? How does Jesus feel in that soul? How would Jesus like to be treated in the soul of the person in front of us?

Jesus would like to be encouraged in that soul. He would like to be strengthened. He would like us to help Him to grow stronger in the soul and to become the Divine Claimant of this soul.

Jesus loves each soul powerfully and totally. We must look at each person as the most cherished child of the Father and we will begin to understand why we must love our neighbor.

This soul in front of us is one that we can help escort through the heavenly gates by our words, our actions, or simply our love.

We must walk gently with the feelings of others, with great reverence for the vulnerability of the spirit. A wounded spirit can be led into all kinds of trouble and we would not like to be the one who has inflicted the wound that caused the downfall of another. Human nature being what it is though, it is possible, indeed probable, that we will hurt others and cause damage to another at some time.

We will come to this realization in silence, not in noise. If upon silent reflection we come to understand that we have hurt another, we should reflect on what Our Lord wishes us to do to assist heaven in healing the wound of the person we have failed. Again, this is not to discourage us, but to cleanse our conscience here on earth, where we can better provide recompense for our failures. It is often the case that our simple admission of wrongdoing can place the person on the path to healing. We should also pray for the healing of the soul so that heaven is invited by us to participate in the righting of the wrong. Heaven heals with far more efficiency than we and the intercessory influence of a repentant soul is powerful. God cannot resist the petitioner who seeks to make amends to others. God comes into these situations with great enthusiasm and effectiveness.

We should not carry the burden of our sin heavily. It is better that we be at peace in our failures while we work with heaven to remove the weaknesses that lead us to sin. We should work steadily with Jesus on our soul, practicing a little holiness each day through the challenges He has placed in front of us. For example, dear apostles, there is no point practicing piety on a day when we are surrounded by souls who annoy us and Jesus is asking us to practice patience. If we follow the path He has traced out for us, we cannot help but become a saint. If we seek to do it our way, we will have greater difficulty.

Always consider kindness. Gentleness and kindness are two attributes that heaven holds in the highest esteem. Our modern world seeks to eradicate these heavenly characteristics but through His apostles Jesus will flood the world with gentleness and kindness.

In order to love our neighbor in the same way as souls love each other in heaven, we must begin to think like residents of that joyful place. In heaven it is all about love and all about Jesus. The Savior, Jesus Christ, is well and truly united to each soul, to the extent that when Jesus enters a room or an area in heaven, nobody remarks upon it because He never leaves any soul. There is constant unity with Christ in the soul. This is available to us here on earth. We are only separated by our lack of faith and lack of commitment to His will. If a soul commits himself to Jesus here on earth, and embarks upward on the mountain path through the service Jesus has willed for the individual, that soul is united to Jesus. Jesus is welcome in that soul and Jesus begins to work through that soul in the unique way that only He could have intended and planned. Each soul has a purpose and the purpose has so many facets over the lifetime of service, or indeed over one day, that we cannot imagine the richness of His plan. But we trust in His plan and that is all that matters. We begin each day by pledging our allegiance to God our Father, and praying the Morning Offering. Then, united to

Jesus Christ in our soul, we step into the day. Jesus works steadily through us all day. His light and love shine to other souls through our actions and words and also in what we do not do and do not say. At the same time as this is happening, Jesus is working on our personal movement up the mountain. He uses each situation, each person, to move us a little further on. So He is working in two ways. He is working in the world, through His ownership of His apostles, both body and soul, and He is working in the soul, through our welcoming of His direction and tutelage. We, the committed apostles, are comfortable with this process because we know that the best plan for us, both in terms of our time on earth and in terms of our time in eternity, is the plan that Jesus has willed. This is what is happening that is invisible and rooted in the spiritual realm of the unseen.

What is the practical reality of this, we might ask. How does an apostle know if he or she is pleasing to God and indeed walking up the mountain path? Well, I can only speak for myself so that is what I will do. When I am serving heaven in unity with the will of the Savior, I feel stretched. I feel a sense that I am laboring. I do not feel a great personal satisfaction characterized by feelings such as "I am truly holy." A more accurate feeling of the apostle ascending the mountain would be "I am truly learning."

We should not dabble in false humility. If we are trying to serve Jesus, we must admit it. And certainly we serve in all of our glorious imperfection, so we must freely admit that as well. We can be open about our commitment to Jesus without being proud of our spiritual advancement or proud of what heaven flows through us. Is a cup proud of the coffee it holds? Does a cup take credit for the quality of the coffee within it? The cup is simply the receptacle or vehicle that is used to transport the coffee from one place to another. A cup is not proud, my friends, and neither should we be.

I began by speaking about love of neighbor and have veered off the track. But the track leads naturally back to the point of entry in that we can love our neighbor purely, like the greatest saint, only if we are willing to do it His way, in unity with Him. All in heaven are willing to assist us, but the heavenly helpers cannot work in a noisy environment. They do so when they must, as in the case of a spiritual emergency, but generally speaking, like good doctors on earth, they need time with their patient in silence and recollection. And it is we, dear apostles, who must be listening with our souls. We must ask heaven to give us the greatest possible love for our neighbor. Heaven will delight in such a request and we will begin to share in the Lord's love for each created soul in the kingdom.

Love of God

There is nothing more instinctive to a soul than the love of God. It is the love of God that propels a soul to the base of the mountain and on up. Apostles should always be alert to the pull coming from the world that draws them in the opposite direction. Anything that draws one away from the ascent pulls one down and progress can be lost. This stated, apostles often get drawn from the mountain or pause in their climb to once again examine what it is that the world is offering them and why it is that they should reject these temptations. This is normal. What is dangerous is when an apostle abandons the mountain altogether, retreating to the glitter and noise offered by the enemy of God. Once surrounded by this noise and glitter, the apostle on holiday from Jesus becomes increasingly more and more deaf to His calls because he has ceased to listen. There are two concerns here.

The first concern is that we do not allow this to happen to us. We should be alert for the following symptoms.

We will begin to be judgmental of our fellow apostles. We will begin to view them as the secular world views them and a spirit of superiority will creep into our consciousness. The mountain path will seem dreary in the extreme and will fill us with revulsion.

Be aware that many laboring apostles periodically view their path with revulsion but they continue the ascent and gradually the feeling passes. There is only one path for us, after all, and if our destination is Jesus, we will only feel confident and at peace on the most direct track to Him.

But this revulsion is different. It is a sneering revulsion and it is quickly followed by a temptation to spend more and more time in the world, enjoying worldly pursuits, even,

God help us, cultivating the admiration of others with regard to our holiness.

There is a coldness that sneaks into this soul as the enemy draws it more and more from the mountain. Do not get caught in this quagmire as one thing leads to another and before we know it we are forced to do all kinds of hard work to disengage ourselves again and get back up to our mountain path. It is this kind of situation that has led to the high number of broken families and interrupted or unfaithful vocations. Understand that as the soul is drawn further and further from the path, the world cheers louder and louder. Heaven speaks in quietness and gentleness, after all, and respects free will. Heaven does not force a soul to compliance. So the further one gets from the path, the louder the world shouts and the less the soul is inclined to listen or hear the warning voices of heaven.

We must not think we will get lured away without our knowledge. We will be making decisions. Sin is not an accident. It is a willful separation from the will of God.

The second concern is in dealing with our fellow apostles who seem to have abandoned their paths. We must be calm and careful in these situations, as we cannot be sure if someone has merely paused to take a breath or is in fact in danger. We will know in this way.

The apostle who is fatigued and who pauses to recommit to the climb will seem discouraged and weary. There will be perhaps some temporary bitterness toward the cross he carries and perhaps some disenchantment with his companions or superiors. This should be treated with all patience and understanding.

The more serious situation, where the apostle has abandoned the climb, will be characterized by a separation from previous spiritual practices, along with behaviors that are not at all consistent with the life of an apostle. Look for a lack of humility here. We should not abandon this soul, of course, and we should gently point out what we have observed. Clearly we must be careful that we do not join him in his rebellion. He will return, with God's grace and our prayers. We must never speak harshly and, again, we should not make judgments. The real risk of separation from God should inspire all apostles to pray for perseverance.

The safest way to proceed is in all obedience to God through His Church on earth. If we look closely, we will see that each decision against the Church, however small in appearance at the onset, can lead to another bigger and potentially more consequential decision later. For example, most abortions begin not at the pregnancy, but at the decision to pursue impure acts with another.

Some will defend their actions by stating that while they respect the Church, they view some Church directives as over the top or unnecessarily strict. Indeed, compared to the licentiousness encouraged by the modern world, much of what the Church asks may be considered too strict.

We must take each moral teaching and follow it all the way down to its furthest possible consequence if ignored. Church positions then make more sense and can be viewed in truth as protective in nature, as opposed to restrictive. Love of God begins with, at least, a respect for the necessity of obedience.

September 29, 2005

I am aware these days that there are those who will attack and quibble with the messenger in order to gain justification for ignoring the message. The message demands a response. It says, "Change your life and do so today, not tomorrow." But not everyone is willing to change their life for Christ so they chip at the messenger. The messenger is none other than a fellow slave of heaven. This is like arguing with the janitor of the castle. You may find fault with the janitor, you may even be able to persuade the janitor that your case has merit, but ultimately the janitor is still the janitor and it is what the king says that goes. So take your case to the King directly and see what He says. If He tells you that the message is flawed and not for you, you should proceed in peace along the path that has been laid out for you, wishing the best of blessings to those who work their patch of ground to serve the King. Anger and bitterness are not fruits of the true Spirit and do nothing to persuade others that you are rooted in the King of Peace.

Love of God is quiet and sure. Those who love God seldom shout others down. It is partially for this reason that evil has flourished in this time as those who represent satan speak loudly and boisterously. They do not listen. They do not judiciously weigh the truth of statements. Rather they seek ways to pierce truth in order to flow falseness through it, thereby blending the two and confusing the faithful.

The faithful must learn to conduct themselves with all calm in this time. We have the kingdom of God in our souls, at our constant beckoning. We need look no further for answers than within. If we do not have the words on our tongue, then we must ask for the Spirit to speak through us and He will do so. Perhaps we will not become eloquent orators who will be known throughout the centuries for our great dissertations. But we will represent our God in all quietness and dignity, if our only statement is the following:

"God is good and I believe in His authority over all mankind."

That statement alone is enough to allow any one of us to

walk away, having done the kingdom the greatest good. The enemy resists God's authority with all rage and bitterness. We must let this rage blow right past us, my friends. The kingdom of God is truly at hand and we will one day see our souls rise to heaven in glory.

There are those who reject His message, stating that the early apostles thought they would see the Second Coming in their time and they did not. This is usually stated with an air of superiority, as if to say, we are far more clever than they. I have many things to say about this.

First, the fact that the Second Coming did not occur in the time of the early apostles is no guarantee that it will not occur in our time. We know it will come sometime because God says it will come. That fact should be enough for us to work with all dedication and zeal, if not for our children, then for our children's children.

Second, if it were to occur today, is there one among us who can say the world is prepared? There is not one among us who can make this statement because the world is not prepared.

Next we must consider whose job it is to prepare the world for the return of the King. Well, I suspect this has fallen to each one of us because it is our time right now. To tell Jesus at our death that we did not work for His return because we did not think it was coming in our time will make us feel foolish. Will we say we thought it would come later so we decided we did not have a compelling role to play despite all of His scriptural urging to the contrary? This is not the position of the lay apostle, of course. It is the position of those who do not wish to serve in completeness.

Finally, is it prudent to wave away the idea of the Second Coming simply because we have been in the end times since the Incarnation? I don't think so. This is similar to saying that because a pregnant woman did not give birth yesterday, she will most certainly not give birth today. The odds are very good that the baby will come someday. It is best to be ready for the inevitable, even if, as it turns out, you will not be the one called upon to deliver the child. Perhaps your job is to help prepare the mother. Jesus is returning. Love of God compels us to help prepare His people.

Think often of what it is about God that is lovable. What comes immediately to my mind is God's acceptance of the humanity that He has created. God accepts us, along with our flaws and mistakes. God is not difficult to please. If all souls understood how little God really wanted from us, there would not be so much resistance to a decision to follow Him.

God is looking for loyalty. He Himself is a loyal friend. Consider what a loyal friend offers. The loyal friend offers constancy. He does not offer and withdraw his friendship. And again offer and withdraw his friendship. The loyal friend is steadfast, even when his friend is in error or at fault. The loyal friend forgives and forgets. But to be a good friend at our end of the relationship, we must admit when we have let God down. This is just and fair. We do not fail our friend and then try to pretend that we did not fail. To do so is to allow the friendship to take a turn toward superficiality and deceptiveness. This is then not a true friendship. This will turn a true friendship into an acquaintanceship, or worse, into a relationship with enmity. So if we fail our friend, we must apologize. Very simple, indeed. If we fail God, we say we are sorry and seek His forgiveness, which is always available.

A difficulty in this time of disobedience is that souls are failing God and then listening to the world, which tells them they are not failing God, because God is unreasonable to expect this loyalty from souls. This trap is as old as mankind.

Didn't the serpent use this temptation successfully against Eve in the garden? No, my friend. Do not be fooled. God is a reasonable God and He asks only for what is necessary to keep us safe and to provide the proper formation for our souls. Love of God extends to loyalty to God and those who speak differently are not seeking the salvation of our souls.

September 30, 2005

Love of God brings calm. In the spirit of defining a thing by moving away from its opposite, I will say that love of the world creates feelings of unrest. There is no point thinking that we will be satisfied in life if our purpose is not God. We will not. We will feel a little anxious, a little disappointed, and a little dissatisfied in our relationships because we will not be appreciated or understood.

Dear friends of the Savior, none of us is completely understood on this earth. Only in heaven will we feel that we are properly appreciated and understood. The difference between those who love God and those who do not is that the lovers of God know that God understands. They sit in silence and in their soul, which they then allow to direct their body and their actions, they know that God understands and God loves them. In gratitude and loyalty, they return that love and accept that they are not properly appreciated and understood on earth. And their bitterness diminishes. The true apostle actually offers Jesus worldly admiration and accepts, in exchange, worldly scorn.

I know that many readers are feeling repulsed by the idea that the world will scorn them. Possibly the next thought is that this is not a holy response to such writings and on the heels of this thought is the thought that perhaps this apostle business is not a good fit for them. I assure each reader that none of us begins by delighting in the scorn of the world. With the help of God, this is where we will end, in a holy detachment from the opinions of others. You see, if we spend our time on earth making decisions that will keep us in the esteem of the world, we will not be serving God to our fullest capability. God is not seeking mediocrity, for all He is forced to accept it. God is seeking exceptional. God is seeking passion. God is seeking a return on the total and selfless love that He has for each one of us. It is this caliber of love that led Him to a violent and humiliating death on the cross. Dear friends, He is entitled to our best in the way of love.

Love of God creates calm in the soul. An apostle who is climbing the mountain will begin to feel calm more often and excited less often. Gradually, sometimes very slowly, the excitability that is constantly fueled by the world will fade as the apostle withdraws from the swirling and retreats into the calm waters of the spiritual realm. This is good. Love of God will encourage this, or rather, demand this, and great progress will follow.

Love of God results in a desire to please Him. We begin to desire to serve Him as He wishes to be served. We want to get it right for Him. The desire to be good and holy is rooted in Christ but initially bears many elements of self-interest. As the soul progresses up the mountain, these elements dissipate and are replaced by more pure motivations.

The apostle who is making progress will sit with Christ in silence and connect to the Lord's disappointment in the non-service and indifference of many souls. In the spirit of consolation, this apostle will make resolutions to distract Our Lord with determined and consistent service. This is a good indication that heaven is uniting the soul to heaven's interests. The more others do not serve, the more this apostle serves. This is in contrast to the early days of the mountain climb when a soul can be pulled into the spirit of non-service easily through association with those who are worldly.

A seasoned apostle, well on the way up the mountain, becomes more committed to the path when he encounters those who are indifferent to his Christ. There is also absent the air of superiority often seen in early climbers. The seasoned apostle understands that he has been given great graces and that he is accountable for these graces. He understands that his holiness is proportionate only to these graces.

The higher one ascends, the less one takes credit for the work that heaven flows through the soul. This is of course because the clarity of the vision increases as one climbs.

I repeat that we must never be discouraged or try to measure our holiness against another's. We must measure our holiness against Jesus Christ. In this way we will remain humble and concentrate not on the road behind us, but on the road in front of us. If the Lord gives us glimpses of His favor, we should thank Him. If He does not, we should not take this as a sign that we are not in His favor. If we are trying to serve and we are living in obedience to our Church, we are sure to make progress.

We should never be complacent. We must understand that if we are alive, there is work to be done in our soul. If we were finished, surely the Lord would have brought us to Him. Work steadily, dear apostles, and we will certainly become as holy as Our Lord requires.

Jesus asks that we begin our day by pledging our allegiance to God the Father. We also pray the Morning Offering. In this way we give Him the day. Jesus states that we should seek His will, which is service to others, rather than the world's will, which is service to self. If this simple advice is followed, our lives will be transformed. A life of selfishness becomes a life of service. We serve, He gives us joy, we become peaceful, and His peace flows through us back into the world. It is like the simplest mathematical equation that is pristine in its soundness.

So the apostle rises and begins to seek opportunities to serve the kingdom. The most obvious and important opportunities will be found in our vocations and these often tedious tasks and services must not be ignored or short-changed because therein lies our primary avenue to holiness and union with God. Joy in service is the motto for a lay apostle.

There is no escaping the cross, of course, and there should be no attempt to escape the service that heaven is asking from us. Some of the promised peace surely must come when we view our life from heaven's point of view and not the world's point of view, which means we will stop *seeking to escape* the service God has willed for us. Joy comes from our willingness because if we are willing there is no resentment.

Consider our day. Consider the tasks that we do not like to complete. Are we discontented and irritated when we are completing these tasks? We must look to heaven and ask if it is heaven asking us to complete these tasks. Perhaps we are asked to complete not only our own work but someone else's work as well. Perhaps our job is made more difficult and our burden is heavier because someone has dumped his or her work and burden on us.

The enemy is looking to exploit this, my friend. Be alert. Understand that because someone else has said "no" to his duty and thereby "no" to God, we are being asked to carry a little extra weight for heaven on this day. We should view this as an opportunity, not a burden. It is clear to me that God is not only asking, but needing His apostles to carry extra weight in this time because so many do not serve.

We are called to do more, it is true, so with God's grace let us do the extra work with a cheerfulness that foils any plans the enemy has to turn us into discontents who add to the unrest in the world.

Discouragement

We must accept that discouragement will come during our mountain climb. If we accept this, we will be less likely to throw up our hands in despair simply because we are a little tired, a little saddened, and a little misused by the world. Our Lord allows this discouragement much like a coach who is interested to see how a team performs under pressure. Also, given that our souls are carried in our bodies, which can be quite noisy in their complaining, we can expect to become discouraged at times.

So how must the lay apostle conduct himself when he is discouraged? Calmly, my friends. Our discouragement does not change anything, least of all our duties. It is often tempting to remain in bed and let the day see to itself. The seasoned apostle rises, discouragement notwithstanding, pledges his allegiance to his God, prays the Morning Offering, steps into the day and begins to serve.

The temptation to stop serving can become serious when levels of discouragement rise. There is an accompanied temptation to stop praying. This is similar to the temptation to stop taking life-saving medicine because of the effort it takes to raise a cup to the lips. It is a foolhardy decision. It is the opposite of prudence. It is like stepping out of a flying plane with no parachute. The odds are against a successful landing with no parachute and the odds are good that our discouragement will interfere with the successful completion of our day if we remove ourself from the reach of heaven and its ministrations. We must pray ourselves through this discouragement and we will join the ranks of the greatest apostles.

You see, our service for the day has been willed by heaven

and heaven has willed this service for us because heaven has need of it. Serve. We should serve when we are discouraged and we will find that the enemy is foiled once again because the enemy is helpless to divert us from our mountain path simply because we are discouraged. This delights the angels and saints.

Scripture gives us plenty of examples of the discouragement of those who have gone before us. I can only imagine how St. Paul felt when he wrote that he and his fellow apostles had been beaten, scorned, imprisoned and slandered. The path up the mountain to the heart of Christ is challenging and the world will not hand us drinks of water on the way up. Rather it will pull at our heels. But heaven will sustain us and heaven will give us the necessary nourishment.

When we greet a day in depression and lethargy, we must simply alert heaven that we are carrying an extra burden. We can then place the burden in our mountain backpack and proceed. We may not feel we are making progress on that day, but heaven will be delighted by our decision to serve regardless and we will get all necessary assistance. If the condition persists, then we should seek the counsel of a trusted priest or a wise fellow apostle.

Discouragement can sometimes come when Our Lord is asking for a change in our course so we must be in constant discussion with Jesus. In this way He can advise us of any upcoming alterations in our course. We will know this because we will begin to determine that the current course is not fruitful for us or for the kingdom. This is quite serious and all due reflection should be given to the consideration of any major course changes.

Those who are ill should not be burdened with the thought that they do not serve. An illness, in and of itself, creates a predisposition for an increase in holiness, and we must not waste the opportunity to suffer with Jesus. This would be like going to the pool on a hot day and staring at the water when we should swim. Better to jump into the heavenly waters of the Trinity and let Them bring our soul to great heights with often dizzying speed.

When someone is ill, that soul can feel he is a burden. Perhaps we are a burden to others because they are forced to think less of themselves and more of others. This can only do them good. Pray for them, that they will not waste the opportunity to also advance in holiness, as this is another situation that predisposes a soul to growth.

If we become ill while on the mountain we will be brought up as though we are on a ski lift. Many souls become ill when they are living for the world and are then carried to the base of the mountain by apostles or, if necessary, by the angels themselves. If they are agreeable to the ministrations of Jesus, He places them on the fast track up to holiness and unity.

Yes, dear fellow apostles, there is a heavenly answer and truth for all experiences on earth. We must not let a little discouragement interfere with Our Lord's plan for our day and for our life. We will be given greater courage if we ask for it and we will wake up tomorrow, if Our Lord chooses to keep us on earth for another day, and we will also serve tomorrow. As the days go by, we will be able to look back on a pattern of heavenly service that allows His kingdom to come through our cooperation. Long live Christ, the Returning King!

Discouragement can come from the enemy. The enemy sometimes attempts to persuade us that our efforts do not bear fruit and that souls are not benefiting from our service to heaven. Very often, to protect our humility, the Lord Himself will conceal the fruits of our efforts. But I am not talking about that here. I am talking instead about the concentrated effort of the enemy of goodness to persuade us to stop our heavenly service by convincing us that our sacrifices are neither appreciated nor effective. This should not sneak up on us because it is such a predictable snare, but alas, it does.

It is here that we need to learn Holy Indifference. This concept, identified by Saint Ignatius of Loyola, allows us to work hard but be detached from the outcome of our efforts. It is enough that Jesus has asked us to complete a task. Our "yes" answers to God give Him the praise and honor He is entitled to. What He brings through our "yes" answers and our efforts is up to Him. The way I see it, this attitude removes us from the enemy's line of fire. If I am acting in good faith, in prayerful obedience to the will of God, I do not need to annoy myself with the outcome of my works. I leave the outcome to Him, who after all is the Director of all service. I may not see the need for an action but I will complete the action. I may not see the benefit of the action I have performed but I commit the act to His divine power and let Him do what He wishes with it. If we proceed in this way, we will be liberated from the outcome of any of our works.

Now in truth and fairness, God seldom asks an apostle to proceed without benefit of any vision of success. Normally God will give us encouragement as we go, but only what is necessary and only what does not interfere with our humility. The higher the altitude on the mountain, the less we may see of the fruits of our efforts. But this will not matter to us in that we will become more trusting in His providence and plan and more willing to work without constant spiritual consolations for the good of the kingdom.

There will be times when all we can say about an act of heroism is that we committed it for love of Christ, such will be the total absence of a visible positive outcome. Well, my dear fellow apostles, let that be enough for us. If an action is committed in honest love and loyalty to Christ, it will have eternal merit that will greet us at heaven's gate.

So when the enemy comes at us, whispering that our service is without benefit to ourself or humanity, we must simply lift up our service to Jesus in loving trust and believe that if the only fruit is the consolation of the tender heart of Jesus, then this will be enough to change the world.

Service to Others

A life lived in Christ will be a life lived in service. When we serve Jesus, we serve humanity, because Jesus Himself is the Servant of all humanity. He came to show us how to live and how to serve.

Jesus did not put Himself above all others. He did not bask in His Kingship, for all it was a divine truth; rather He worked hard according to His state in life, as a carpenter and then as an evangelist. Our Lord viewed His apostles with love and understanding. He considered that each was in a different place on the mountain and He treated them as individuals, according to their spiritual capabilities. He does the same for us and we must do the same for others. The lay apostle must be gentle in his service to others.

We understand that the first will be last and the last will be first in that those who push themselves forward for special treatment are necessarily pushing others behind them. This is not the Christian way, of course. If my reader will pardon my attempt to extend this out in a concrete way, I will pursue this thought.

We accept that we are to be the servants of others. In the simplest terms, we opt to be the one who is in the kitchen preparing the food and then cleaning up after the feast. This is good and this is the idea. Well done if we are here. But let's look not only at the service but also at the spirit of the service.

We opt to cook and clean and do so in union with Christ, and in great love and prayer for the others who are not serving but enjoying the party. Well done again and even better if we are here.

Conversely, cooking and cleaning resentfully is not the idea. If we are here, we must ask Jesus to fill us with love for those we serve. Let's move a bit further.

We opt to cook and clean in union with Jesus, in prayerful petitioning for the ones enjoying the party. Those souls are ridiculing and mocking us for the very service we perform. They show us that they feel superior to us and even treat us with pitying disrespect. Because our service shines a light on their non-service and exposes them, they strike out at us in their guilt. They deliberately misunderstand our motives, which wounds us terribly.

We take this and offer it to Jesus in union with His Passion for these very souls and beg Him for conversion graces and clarity for them. We feel the stings but soldier on, overcoming any urges to retaliate by showing them that we are not fools to be taken advantage of, but willing victims for heaven. We correctly see these urges as temptations to be overcome.

This is very good and if we are not here, we must be at peace, as we will surely arrive at this destination if we have the desire.

We cannot discuss service without remarking on the self-imposed or self-assigned martyrdom of many apostles on the hill. Please, let us not be martyrs unless we are quite certain that Jesus is in fact requesting this of us. We must not take our service and rebuke others with it. This defeats two purposes, which are the advancement of our own holiness and the example and love we give to others.

Yes, we are all guilty of self-inflicted and enjoyable martyrdom at some time and that is why we must look closely and identify this as a trap that can turn us into a Pharisee.

Some will cook and clean simply as a reproach to others, to hold themselves above others. They use their service as evidence of their holiness, and not contenting themselves with this mistake, they use their service further as evidence that others are unholy. Oh, dear. This is all wrong. It is far better, my fellow apostle, if we remain in the celebration and leave the service to others if our motives are those of self-promotion. As Scripture says, we will be enjoying our reward on earth, not in heaven. A bigger risk is that others will be turned away from Christ, whom we represent, because souls will falsely see Christ as Someone who is judgmental and prideful as opposed to tolerant and humble. We represent Christ to others, after all, and it is good to understand that Christ always served in the spirit of love.

Always complete acts of service in a good spirit, with an awareness, not of the failings of others, but of our own failings. A healthy sense of humor will help us to laugh at our ridiculousness in this area.

We must always be alert to the distorted reasoning promoted by the enemy so I want to caution that we should not refrain from all service because we have mixed motives. If we are identifying mixed motives, we are well on the way to eradicating them and purifying them with the help of Christ.

So let us look closely at our motives, asking Jesus to make them pure, as we continue on always in service. Serve, serve, and serve. The lay apostle in this time, and indeed in every time, must work very hard to compensate for those who are not serving. The harder we work, the more graces obtained and the greater the number of apostles who are pulled into the mission. We cannot fail.

Joy in Service

This may be the single most important topic that is covered. When a soul is performing a service for Jesus, generally great joy is available to accompany the work. If this joy is accessed, others will see heaven. It is that simple. When one proceeds through life, even during hardship, united to Jesus and in the awareness of heaven's presence, there is joy. Others see this and cannot help but notice and become affected by the joy of the true apostolic servant.

During this time there is an absence of joy, as well as a dearth of service. It is for this reason that we are immersed in a self-perpetuating darkness. Souls do not serve, others remain unloved and fall into darkness and they in turn do not serve and others remain unloved and on it goes.

Just as non-service is contagious, so also is service. Joyful service is even more contagious because in a time when so few experience joy, there is a premium on it, so much so that the world makes constant claims about this thing or that thing, all offering joy. In the west, it is materialism. Souls are told that if they own this car or those shoes they will have joy. We have turned into a world filled with lords and masters. There is a shortage of true servants, but now the lay apostle will reverse this trend with his dedicated service to Jesus Christ, his Returning King.

So how do we obtain joy in service? We must understand that everything we do in a day, we do with and for Jesus Christ. He is in us. He is with us. If we are cleaning our car, washing our dishes, surviving a contentious meeting or caring for a loved one, we do so in unity with Him. He is never apart from us. He wants to speak to us each day, all day. He has a goal and purpose for each task we perform. All of heaven has an interest in our willing completion of every chore, every service.

Jesus is grateful to us for every chore and every service. When we unite each action in our day to Him, He uses each action to restore peace in the world by exchanging our willingness and service for heavenly graces.

Someone once lamented disunity in parishes, in churches, and between holy organizations. They asked what they could do about it. Well, on any given day, if I mop my floor and prepare meals for my family in a spirit of cheerful willingness, I am creating unity and harmony between those in other areas of the world. Jesus may use my floor mopping to create peace between two families in Tibet or two warring parish councils. Jesus may use the farmer's labors to restore unity to a tribe in a remote area we have never heard about or in the city council of our hometown. The lay apostle must believe that his daily service is fueling the renewal. The lay apostle must believe this because it is true.

Do not be one who reflects constantly on the dreadful state of the world. It cannot be all that bad as Jesus is here and angels and saints surround us. Earth is an extension of heaven, dear apostles. I know with certainty that Jesus is within me. And I am here, on earth. And earth is God's creation. So it is wrong to proceed with a long face. There are souls to be loved and services to be performed.

Do not reflect constantly on the dreadful state of the world because by doing so one spreads the fruits of darkness, fear and despair. Be one who reflects constantly on the joyful state of heaven. That is our final destination after all and all is well in heaven. All will be well when we arrive there. We are here for a short time and we are given the opportunity to do our little bit to improve matters for others, so, within our precious vocations, let us proceed to do that for Jesus. When we proceed through our lives in unity with Jesus, we have joy, even in hardship. Suffering is quite a different matter when there is a purpose and meaning attached to it. Now, to be honest, we must admit that the lay apostle cannot always be joyful, even though he may try to be joyful and desire to be joyful. This should not discourage us. In the absence of joy, insert cheerfulness, because this is another contagious condition. On some days, all that we may have to give Jesus is forced cheerfulness.

I will make this promise to each reader. If the reader pretends to be cheerful long enough, he will become cheerful, even when he is unhappy. If I am wrong about this, the reader can tell me about it in heaven at the greatest length and I will cheerfully listen and accept responsibility.

October 5, 2005

The reason the apostle can experience joy in service is this. In heaven, all souls are in unity with the divine will. There is no conflict, no tugging at the will by the appetites of the body or by the lust for worldly possessions. Souls in heaven have relinquished their wills in that they experience God's love and commit themselves to Him once and for all, in the greatest joy and gratitude and wisdom. They get it. They finally get it and it gives them great peace. They become residents of that heavenly kingdom and know no more anger, pain, distress, hurt, envy, fear, anxiety, or greed. On they go to live in peace with others, exploring the kingdom, learning about the exploits and triumphs of others, and exulting in each other and in the vast creation that is the universe.

An apostle working for Christ has begun the mountain climb and necessarily has relinquished some of his will, saying "no" to bodily appetites and overcoming some of his desire to accumulate worldly possessions. This rejection of self-will puts the apostle into the realm of the divine.

There is great joy in heaven, always. When the apostle begins this climb and rejects self-will, he is saying "yes" to the calling of his soul. This gives him a foretaste of heaven and encourages him to do more and more and climb higher and higher.

Joy in service is really the opposite of selfishness. Moving further away from that negative pole, joy in service is living for the soul and not the body, or living for God and not self. Perhaps I belabor this point. I do so because it is fundamental Christianity and this point is what will eventually allow us to be at home in heaven. This point is what will push us up the mountain like a strong wind at our backs. Service to others is the beginning of freedom from self-gratification.

I wonder if there is an apostle who asks why God gave us this heavily weighted body to escape from. Truly, it is burdensome in the extreme if we consider that we are constantly fighting with it and trying to overcome its demands, which claw at us and drag us away from possessing our soul. I find that the more I learn about the soul, the more I wish to free myself from the body so I can live only for the soul. I am patiently fed up with the demands of my body and yet I understand that my body must be respected and cared for so that it can carry Jesus to others while my soul remains in it.

And I suppose that is the answer really. Our Lord and God has willed that we spend this time in exile, in service. I have the smallest experience of heaven and the souls there are filled with love, filled with Jesus. Well, if a soul rejected Christ, which is his choice, he would not fit in with the residents of heaven. He would not be at home there. The point is that we are here to choose God or not to choose God. The extent that we choose God determines the extent of the goodness God can flow through us here on earth.

As we climb the mountain higher and higher toward heaven, our soul becomes stronger and its capacity to hold Christ becomes greater. We begin to disappear and Christ radiates through us. The higher we climb, the more Christ controls our will. This is done with our permission, lest souls begin to fear this heavenly possession. Souls in heaven are very much themselves, only they are themselves united to Christ. Can there be anything more desirable or beautiful?

I have to say that if Christ possessed me, others would be safe from me and I could do no damage. If Christ possessed me, there would be no way that the enemy could use me to glorify himself or his legion of bitter ones. If Christ possessed me, His light would flow through me in a constant stream of grace and love. We must desire this unity above all else. Perhaps we will not reach that point on earth, but we will continue to offer Jesus our willingness and see what He can do with us.

We will find joy in service because we will begin to experience heaven in saying "no" to self and "yes" to Him.

Joy in service takes many forms. It comes on quietly, so much so that the soul does not always identify it. It feels like satisfaction and peace. It creeps up on the soul working for Christ and that soul finds himself gradually more peaceful than anxious. The soul working for the kingdom is moving forward steadily. This stated, much as a rower does not always see progress in the short term, the apostle often does not see either the fruit of his labor or the progress of his soul. The rower keeps his head down and keeps rowing, despite wind and fatigue. The rower often takes his eyes from the destination and the satisfaction begins to come from the labor itself. You see, the rower's muscles are growing with each pull and the initial aches and pains disappear, leaving a rower well able for the task.

The experienced apostle working for Christ no longer considers whether or not the destination is close. He does not consider what he is gaining from the service. He just knows he has to serve. All is left up to Christ. The apostle making progress on the mountain overlooks the difficulty of the climb and steps constantly over and around obstacles. He no longer considers obstacles as something that indicate a change in course, but as something that must be traversed.

Fatigue is expected on the mountain and fellow apostles distract each other with their joy, often noting the glory of the destination for the apostle who has collapsed in discouragement. Truly, it is a great gift to have holy companions on this journey up the mountain and we must thank God if He has allowed this for us. If He has not allowed this for us, thank Him again because it means He is jealous of our heart and wants to keep it mostly for Himself. If we understand that all comes from Him, we will think less of being relieved from any of it. We will think more of managing our crosses in holiness and acceptance.

For my own clarification, let me say it this way.

I am walking up the mountain carrying my backpack of flaws, faults, and failings, which add weight to my climb. The more I get a handle on those, the less weight in my pack.

Additionally, I have the weight from any crosses Jesus has given to me. Consider the crosses this way. Each cross is like a precious stone we are delivering to Jesus. The heavier the weight of the cross, the more beautiful and valuable is the gem that we will hand Him. Perhaps we may decide that one of these crosses we will carry for Mary, our beloved mother, and that will be a beautiful gem for her to be blessed with and enjoy. When we give it to her, she will take it and with it she will obtain the graces to ransom back ten thousand souls. Now the ten thousand is an arbitrary number so please don't say that Anne guaranteed you ten thousand souls for carrying the cross of say . . . psoriasis. I don't know the number, but I know this.

Jesus Christ is far more generous than our wildest dreams can imagine. Our Lady has far more power than our wildest dreams can imagine. God lets her do pretty much what she wants. Why wouldn't He? Mary's will matches His to perfection. She is simply carrying out what He wants. But she goes at problems in a feminine way, filled with feminine mercy and armed with the heavy weaponry of God's gratitude to her. Souls underestimate the power of the mother.

But these gems get heavy. That does not mean we do not want to deliver them to Jesus. It just means that sometimes we have to rest a little. But generally, if we carry our gems cheerfully up the hill, we will not be sorry. There is great beauty and value in our crosses, dear apostles. Based on the value of each soul, the value of the cross we carry is priceless.

And we are saving souls. Believe it because it is true. Therein lies a portion of our joy in service.

Love of Jesus

October 6, 2005

It is like every honor in the world to be asked to write about love of Jesus. Where does one begin and more importantly, how does one finish a task such as this? One will never be finished. That stated, when asked to do something, it is best to begin.

Love of Jesus is like the wind. We cannot see it, we cannot always identify its origin, but it has great impact on us and can actually alter our course. It can begin in softness, as a gentle stirring, and end in the greatest of storms that will lead us to heroic deeds and action. Love of Jesus brings us to the base of the mountain.

What is first experienced is the love Jesus has for us. Our love of Christ is actually a response to His perfect love for us because His love always was and always will be. The love between a soul and his Savior is a reciprocal thing.

God's love must be entertained by the soul in order to grow. If the soul has a heart surrounded by ice, Jesus will melt that ice, but He can only work if He is allowed. This ice, the result of sin and of the wounds inflicted by the world, closes off the divine. The heart needs love like the lungs need oxygen. Our Lord Himself has said this. So the more closed the heart is to the divinity, the less capable it is of loving. A soul can sometimes rest in mortal sin or in the world for a long period. This heart becomes hardened and toughened. The longer the heart is closed off to Christ, the more accustomed the soul becomes to living without the love of Christ. This stated, the Divine Healer needs only the smallest crack and He can flood the soul with warmth and heat, melting the ice and restoring the heart to a condition where it can freely give and receive love from Jesus and from other souls.

The love of Christ is the most powerful driving force on earth. It is what compels souls to service. It compels souls to work tirelessly for others, their brothers and sisters who are also beloved by Jesus. This is because when we love someone, we begin to accept their goals as our own. If nothing else, we understand the goals of the beloved and if we can help to further those goals, we will do so. We will always have one eye on what is happening to the plans of our beloved. It is this way for all souls who love each other in the world and it is this way for the apostle who loves Jesus Christ.

The more we come to know Jesus, the more we love Him.

This is a truth that needs no other explanation but it is so important it bears repeating.

The more we come to know Jesus, the more we love Him.

If a soul has correctly identified the mountain as the direction he must take, yet he feels no compelling or passionate love for Jesus Christ, he must ask for this immediately. This soul must lose no time in taking a course in the love of Christ. This is good advice, dear fellow apostles, so heed it well. We must ask Jesus to make Himself known to us. The lay apostle seeks to live following the example of kindness set out by Jesus Christ as illustrated in Sacred Scripture, so Sacred Scripture is the place to begin.

Consider Jesus on earth, the Man with a soul that rests in God and is God. This God has agreed to trap His soul, as it were, in the limitations of the body like one of His created ones on earth. He walks this earth and lives a life as a Man but with divine knowledge and awareness. Jesus Christ was acutely aware that He was here to set an example. And that is the first thing we must always consider in our days. We, like

Christ, are setting an example. Are our daily actions an appropriate example to others?

We should read Scripture and soak up everything Jesus said and did because it was all intended to show us exactly how to live and how to love each other. When we read about Him, considering what He must have been thinking and what He must have been feeling, we will fall for Jesus more and more, as so many have before us.

Love of Jesus is as natural as breathing for a child of God. It is personal to Him and we must make it personal to us. Talk to our Jesus often during the day. Ask Him what He was thinking as He experienced the most life choking dread in the Garden of Gethsemane. We must ask ourselves what we would be thinking were we in His place.

I can understand that the Passion was beyond dreadful. What I cannot imagine is how He survived the anticipation of it. There was nowhere to run and no escaping it.

Imagine saying to God, "Any chance I can avoid this?" That was the hypothetical, nearly panicked plea of a human about to experience unthinkable cruelty. He knew full well there was no chance. He had signed on for this Redemptive Act of all Acts and He was not the kind to go back on a decision made in love for others and destined to secure our salvation. So, because He loved us personally and passionately, He offered Himself up to be savaged.

Dear apostles, we should each consider this for a period of time today and even if we have never felt love for Jesus before, we will feel it today.

When we love someone we begin to look at the world through their eyes, as I have said. Their perspective is always with us. When we look at the world through the eyes of Jesus, we can feel His pain because so many souls do not know about

His love. They are troubled. Troubled souls can be hurtful. Loving Jesus has forced me to view souls differently. It is clear that a soul who is wounded needs the healing love of Jesus. But this soul may be angry at Jesus. We have talked before about the Centurion not identifying Jesus as the Son of Man until AFTER Jesus suffered at his hands. Love of Jesus makes it a lot more bearable to be mistreated by others. In fact, we begin to understand that the treatment we suffer from souls on earth has nothing to do with how Christ views us. Souls may be disrespectful and feel superior. Love of Christ turns this experience into fellowship with Christ, as this is how He was treated. As we make progress up the mountain, we begin to expect this treatment, we think less of rebelling against this treatment and defending ourselves, and we see that being treated thus for Christ puts us into a group of wonderful apostles.

Love of Christ also creates the joy in service that is so important to apostles. When we serve alongside Christ or with Christ within us as a guide and friend, it is different than service to the world or service for the support or sustenance of our family. There is a divine purpose and the daily walk with Jesus confirms us in all we do.

I am having some difficulty, much to Our Lord's disappointment I am sure, so I will revert back to my experience of Jesus. I love Him so much that I want to do anything for Him. It pleases me to please Him. I see the world and I understand that Jesus loves each soul as much as He loves me. And yet, some do not know Him. Some know Him but reject Him. Some, and I say this with all gravity, work against our sweet Jesus. This is a dreadful situation indeed. This hurts Jesus and I feel that because this hurts Jesus, it must hurt me. I realize there are souls saying, "Well yes, she may be right, but it has always been this way." Well, that may be true. But it has not always been my job to do something about it. During this time in history, it is my job, and the job of each lay apostle.

Again, there is no point discussing what occurred in someone else's time or what may occur in the future when we are gone. This is our time. We are called to work now. Souls are in darkness now, at this moment, and we have the power from Jesus to touch them and bring Jesus to them. There is no wriggling out of this responsibility. If we love Jesus at all, we must work for souls.

October 7, 2005

Love of Jesus moves through everything we do as apostles. Love of Jesus becomes a living thing. Again I reference breathing, which is not usually a conscious act, but a reflexive necessity. All things end at love of Jesus and all things begin there. We admire a tree that is particularly graceful. Love of Jesus is in that admiration because Jesus is God and God is the Creator. Love of Jesus, for the apostle, is something that is ongoing. This love wraps everything in one package, our life, which He will someday present to the Father. Love of Jesus is good and we should ask Jesus for more of this love each day.

For a period of time, let us ask ourselves to view each soul and each situation and consider how Jesus views it. For example, at the beginning of our day, survey the first task and see what Jesus thinks about it.

I look in at a messy kitchen, which has survived the ravages of the children who blow through it quickly en route to another school day. I ask myself how Jesus sees this kitchen.

Well, He sees the mess, certainly, as a task to be completed in unity with Him. But He sees also the imprint on this room of each little soul in his formation. He sees the interactions that occurred between the children and the parents. He sees the gentle course corrections, the breaches of peace, and then the peace restored. He sees all the teaching that went on in one uneventful morning's breakfast rush. When viewed through His eyes, this kitchen looks different. It is one morning, which will be added to the tapestry of each family member's entire life.

I clean and pray for each child, that they will walk with Jesus always and learn from Him how to live. I know that they do this through our example as parents and I consider where I need to improve. I pray for Jesus to help me to do better as I clean. I pray for Jesus to bless my day and flow through me as I proceed. I ask Him to alert me to my failings so that I do not do any damage to the goals of the kingdom on this day. I beg Jesus to allow me to advance in holiness so that I can manage what He has put in front of me. I think of the souls in purgatory and ask for their relief. I look at my card of special intentions and ask Jesus to look in on each of them. I glance at my Divine Mercy image and ask God to have mercy on the whole world. This is just the kitchen. And look at what Jesus can do if I give Him the act of cleaning the kitchen. I do this because I love Him.

Now there are also bad days, when I clean without thinking, mindful only of the cross I am carrying. On that day, Jesus looks at my kitchen a little differently. I see perhaps the failings, the impatience with the morning's rush and the spilled milk, undone homework, and loud fights among the children. Nothing seems to be going well on this day. The last thing I want to do is clean this kitchen with its memory of my failings. But how does Jesus see it?

On this day, this kitchen is my little Calvary. With the greatest courage I must wade into it with Christ, praying for strength or simply praying that Jesus will take away any bitterness that has crept into my soul. Understand of course, that my kitchen could be your boardroom, or your service in a hospital, or as a bus driver, or in front of a computer screen. Our kitchen is the daily work Our Lord is asking us to complete.

Compare the difference between working with Christ and working with the enemy. The enemy will tell us that it is not fair that we should have to clean our kitchens. He will sow seeds of discontent and bitterness. He will remind us of past hurts and try to reopen wounds that should be long healed. The enemy will show us the flaws in our lives and if we turn on the television, the enemy will show us how other souls are vacationing in small bathing suits, while we are covering stretch marks and sweeping floors again. The enemy will complain about our little ones and our husbands or wives, if we are lucky enough to live in an intact sacramental union that is not abusive. The devil will say that the families we serve do not appreciate us and on any given day this may be true. But we are walking with Jesus Christ and Jesus Christ appreciates us.

It is important to walk with Christ in our day if only to reject the enemy. Jesus sees our courage as we accept the cross that is ours and carry it with Him. He sends additional courage when necessary and lets us cry with Him when we need to cry. He has all the time in the world and He cares for each one of us as though we were His only friend. He puts love in our hearts and courage in our souls. Love of Jesus puts us in His presence in everything and we live differently in His presence.

Most of us complain at times. But there are apostles on the mountain who do not complain and Jesus loves them most tenderly. Let Jesus give us the grace to follow in their footsteps and catch up to them. Until then, Jesus will help us to grow in holiness as a reward for our willingness to be humble and accepting of both our cross and our failings.

One day I felt the cup of bitterness overflowing. I was saturated with bitterness and this resulted in anger. Knowing that

I needed to be alone, I obtained a precious period of time and set out for a long, pounding walk. I passed the Adoration Chapel, trying to move quickly as the last thing I wanted to do was pray. To be honest, I was angry at Jesus because I was convinced that heaven was unreasonable in its expectations. I wanted to walk hard and deal with all that was hurting me.

Jesus said, *"Come to Me, Anne."*

I said, "No, Lord. Trust me. You do not want me in this condition. I am too mad."

He replied, *"Fine. Walk with My enemy instead."*

I made the sharpest turn you can imagine. I understood that the enemy was gleeful at my condition and was more than willing to entertain me with all of the wrongs that had been sent my way and all of the injustices present in the work Jesus had willed for me. It was the enemy who had whipped me into this condition. My friends, the enemy had set me up.

I went into Adoration and sat down hard and began to complain. I complained and I complained. I left nothing out. And Jesus listened. And He listened some more.

At the end of thirty minutes of complaining, I glanced at Him in the Host. He was so pure, so kind, and so tolerant that my heart melted. He had let me get it all off my chest. What healed me was His perfect love and charity for me. My love for Him gushed out of my soul. I was a different person at the end of that hour than I would have been after a walk with the enemy who wished to encourage me in rebellion. I left Jesus like a lamb, willing to be hurt in service to Him for the sake of others. We must never underestimate what Jesus can do for us and we should understand that Jesus will take us in any condition.

My love for Jesus is all wrapped up in my gratitude to Him. I am grateful to Jesus because He has forgiven me of all of my sins and healed me.

Jesus bestows dignity on every soul. Each soul created by the Father has a divine purpose and each soul created by the Father is the Father's treasure. The world seeks to strip dignity from humanity. As apostles, we must be always aware of this effort by God's enemy. This dignity-stripping attempt manifests in many ways. The most obvious is abortion. Less obvious is birth control. Consider what contraception has taken from us.

Contraception has taken a huge measure of dignity from women, men and children. Children are viewed as something to be avoided. Women are viewed as sex partners. Pregnancy is treated like a disease and men are so confused they are not sure what being a man means anymore. Many young men and women do not understand that they can and should say "no" to premarital sexual activity. Why would they understand this when everywhere they turn they are being handed birth control? They are being encouraged to have sex. This hurts Jesus.

Our love for Jesus insists that we work against this message. Women were not created by God to be exploited. Children are God's treasure and our future. And men deserve the dignity that comes with responsible governing of their sexual desires. God's created plan is beautiful. The enemy's distortion of this plan can be seen, in all its ugliness, in contraception and abortion.

The lay apostle is called to live chastely, according to his state in life. We must always be aware of the mountain path and what can pull us from it. Clearly lay apostles are called to be faithful to our Church and our Church, reflecting God's will, reflects God's plan that sexual intercourse be reserved for those in a blessed union. Again it is a symptom of the darkness that so many say "no" to their vocations. The number of priests and sisters is down not because Jesus decided that having priests and sisters was a bad idea but because souls, often lacking formation, stopped accepting God's invitation to their vocations.

The same thing is happening with marriages. Many souls are living together without the benefit of marriage. They are saying "no" to the vocation of being a husband or wife. They are living together and acting as husbands and wives but without the blessings reserved for the sacramental marriage. If a family is based on the solid ground that is a blessed union, God can send all manner of graces and also mitigations for the flaws of the parents and children. He compensates for our failings. But in many cases today children are being brought up, not in families, but in worldly partnerships. This is bad for the father, mother, and the children.

Another symptom of this age is the acceptance of homosexuality as an alternative life style. It is an alternative, yes. It is a bad alternative to a holy lifestyle and it is not something that can or should be sanctioned by souls who work for Jesus Christ. We must be courageous when we represent God's will in this matter. We must not be bullied. The kingdom of God needs every soul working and each soul is critical to the Second Coming. We cannot afford to lose souls to the lie that our brothers and sisters can live in a sinful and rebellious manner and still be working for Christ.

If each soul will look deeply into the eyes of his God, he will understand that God does not wish anyone to continue on this rebellious path. Every soul is called to be chaste, according to his state in life. We will each face God some day and His truth will be right in front of us, impossible to ignore. Lay apostles must encourage all souls to stop ignoring this dangerous deceit. Brothers and sisters, we are losing souls to this. We must push back hard on this issue.

We must all join in prayer that the Church will respond

appropriately to the needs of so many of our fellow apostles who have been affected by divorce. We are all acutely aware that many souls wish to be in blessed unions or wish to be freed from unions that are not sacramental. We bring this to Jesus in trust that just as we love Him, He loves us and sees our needs. We also bring Him our youth, again in great trust, and ask that He help us to see our roles clearly so that we can proclaim His truths.

October 8, 2005

Who can turn away from the love of Christ? Jesus loves with such acceptance. Living in unity with Jesus is like having the most perfect friend. He will never judge us harshly. Jesus sees our motives and understands that often we fail as the result of the wounds that have been inflicted on us. A treasured friend is this way and helps us to deal with our mistakes charitably because the close friend has been with us in our past and views us as a whole, made up of a lifetime of experiences. A treasured friend can usually guess what we will do in a given situation and this is the same with Jesus. Jesus allows us to be tried and He allows us to fail, often so that we will learn.

There is a story about a hole in the road. A child steps into the hole repeatedly until, after many consequences, he learns to walk around the hole, and finally begins taking another street and avoiding it altogether. Well, this is how it is for us at times. Which one of us can say that we have not repeated a mistake? The God we love understands that it can take repeated lessons until we learn. If Jesus accepts us with such readiness, can it be right that we judge ourselves harshly?

We are called to emulate Him. He is tolerant of us. Dear apostles, let us accept our humanity and our flaws in the same way that Jesus accepts them. There is a snare that has tripped up many before us and I will tell you about it. We have all suffered in our past, often being forced to experience the consequences of our own frailties and flaws. We have also been forced to suffer from the frailties and flaws of those around us, often in our families. Those experiences leave wounds, as we have discussed. Those wounds lead us to strike out at times in ways that are sinful or painful. We have all heard remarks about someone who is working against himself. Or again, that someone is his own worst enemy.

This self-destructive attitude or pattern of thinking can be a cop-out. We do not want to fall into this trap, so let us all be alert here. Do not think that because you have made mistakes you are not called to work with Jesus Christ. Further, do not think that because others have hurt you, and these wounds have perhaps placed you on a path of pain and self-destructive behavior, that you will be exempt from service to heaven. When you die, you will wish you had served. Let us be certain that we are not excusing ourselves from heavenly service by citing past injury.

To be perfectly clear, and possibly belabor the point, do not think, Well, if God wanted me to serve He should not have let me be hurt by these others. The world has been unfair to me so too bad. Or the most belligerent, God doesn't care about me, so I don't care about Him. This is childish and dangerous thinking and it will not land us in a good place. I am not threatening hell here, dear friend. That would be a bit beyond the scope of my mission. I am warning that we will have the most excruciating regrets for having rejected His love. And He does love us, far more than we can possibly understand. He sees each of our hurts and wounds and wants to heal them. He can restore us in a blink and put us on a path to perfection and joy. But we must come to Him. We must repent of OUR mistakes and leave the mistakes of others to Jesus. He will deal with those who have hurt us far more effectively than we can.

To say it another way, let us never blame others for our actions. Let us never point to the sins of others and use these human sins as proof of God's malice or indifference. Let us never say that Jesus has rejected us and use that as our reason for not serving. Let us never try to escape from service by saying we have nothing to give or that we are of no value to heaven. Again, this will not work for us at our death. This type of rebellion grieves Jesus terribly and is a good indication of the spiritual company we are keeping. It will not work for us when we leave our bodies and look back on our lives in the presence of God. Believe me please when I say that we will want some kind of service to give to God.

Love of Divine Will

October 10, 2005

We should always be conscious of the separation between our personal will and God's will. Sometimes there is the smallest distance between the two and sometimes there is a chasm so wide and deep between them that we wonder what God is thinking. The answer is that it is God's business what He is thinking and our business to cross the divide. We must always, each day, spend a few minutes in silence to determine if we are on the correct side of that canyon. Between the two wills is a nowhere land. Most apostles will find themselves in nowhere land at times, but most particularly at the beginning of the climb.

The will of God can be repugnant to us if we are not aligned to it. We are all familiar with the prayer of gentle coercion. This prayer is one in which we explain our will to Jesus in the hope that we are talking Him into it. We will always include a section that tells God why our plan would work for Him too. We show God the heavenly benefits we think He can extract from our plan and cross our fingers. Happily, God is not an easy sell. He knows what He needs from us and He knows our capabilities. He has marked out a path that accommodates both of these things. This is the best possible path for us.

How does one know if one is following God's will in his life? Unless one spends time with God in silence, it will be difficult. We must give God the time to reveal His will to us each day. Generally speaking, there are clues that we have left the divine will and entered into the nowhere land or, more seriously, crossed the divide entirely and embarked upon a path marked out by ourselves, leading further in to the world.

When we are following the divine will there is a feeling of peace. This peace will withstand temptation, attack, obstacles, and criticism. When others disdain us or ridicule us, it is uncomfortable. When God is disappointed in us, it is unbearable, but only if we are paying attention and only if we care. If a soul is determined to depart from the divine will, Christ will not stop the soul. How could He, given His gift of free will? Again, it will help us to discern if we look for symptomatic evidence.

In consideration, do we feel a sense of humility? Are we aware of our gross limitations without Christ and the graces He flows through us? Do we often marvel at our nothingness, along with what seems to be accomplished through us despite this nothingness? Do we carry always a sense of what sin we are capable of if left to our own devices? Are we fearful at times that we are not serving as completely as we should? Do we have a consistent feeling that we would like to do better for Him and that we should do better for Him?

This is good, dear apostles. We must rest in these thoughts because without Him we are nothing. If left to our own devices, we could easily lapse into the sinful patterns of our past, along with new sins besides. Humility is the closest friend of the apostle and if we take humility for granted it will go away. Be assured that God is great and that without Him we are nothing. The greater the good and the greater the graces He manages to flow through us, the more we should understand His majesty.

Conversely, if we have left the divine will, we may have put our fingers in our ears so that we cannot hear Him. This is not unheard of and most of us have done this at some time in our lives. We will remember it as a feeling of restlessness with sparks of bitterness and anger. There will be feelings of defiance sprinkled with the idea that heaven is unreasonable and that the demands of heaven are pressing harder against us than against others.

On the heels of this we may reach the land of superiority, which is an ugly place to rest. Our eyes looking at others from this location hold no love, only indifference, repugnance or judgment. When we have drifted over the chasm, we need a sharp tug to pull us back. Remember that the further we go into nowhere land, the further we get from the mountain. The voice of the world becomes louder. The voice of God, the Gentle One, who does not force us, becomes less distinct.

I must stress here, lest souls make a mistake, that God is not to blame for our departure from His will. He has not let go of us, like a hot air balloon. We are in charge of where we attach ourselves. If we are drifting, there will be symptoms. The best way to be sure that we remain in the divine will is to remain always close to Jesus by always facing Him and facing up to the top of the mountain. If we turn and face the world, we begin to think we are just dandy, given our altitude. Facing the perfection of Christ keeps us clear on exactly how far we have to go until we reach perfection.

The way in which we continue to face in His direction, upward, is through prayer. We must always remind ourselves that our soul needs constant nourishment, just as our body needs constant nourishment. How often do we forget to eat? Well, we should treat prayer the same way. We must be faithful to our daily prayer commitments and we will remain anchored in the land of the divine will.

When discerning the divine will in our lives, it is good to have a place to begin. We begin with sin.

It can never be the will of God that we commit sin. At the same time, we can stipulate to the fact that we will all commit sin. Given this, we must keep connected to the cleansing method God has given us through our Church, which is the Sacrament of Penance. There are so many graces available to us in this sacrament that if we could see these graces visually, we would take full advantage of any opportunity to obtain them.

When an apostle is climbing the mountain, he makes mistakes. The higher the altitude, the higher the standard of behavior. Most apostles on the mountain will not be stealing candy bars and yet some souls stopped their participation in this sacrament at that level. Let us consider a mistake as a choice for our will over God's will and begin with the Ten Commandments. We should be living in accordance with those commandments.

Some of us have seen ten or twenty or thirty years elapse from our last Confession. If this describes us, we must remedy the situation at once and seek God's forgiveness and healing by going to Confession. In this way we obtain the graces we need to correctly discern God's will from our will and also to correctly identify when we have abandoned God's will for our will.

God has truly thought of everything. Our God knows us inside and out and He knows what we need. My dear fellow apostles, we agree to go to Confession once each month in deference to God and to our apostolate, but it is we who draw the benefits from keeping this agreement. Let us be faithful to this so that we allow our God to cleanse and nourish us.

Sometimes God needs something from us that we do not want to give. This is the cold hard reality so we may as well consider it. How often have we had a thought, a prompt from heaven and been filled with revulsion saying, "God, I just pray you are not going to ask me to do that!" The request does not go away, regardless of how hard we try to dodge it or forget about it or talk ourselves or God out of it. God remains still and the request stands.

I understand, my friends, how this feels. How can I console a fellow apostle who is feeling terrific repugnance to the situation that God has placed him in? This is a little bit like jumping into cold water. If you have to swim, you have to swim. God's will should always triumph in His apostles. We want this and we know we want it because we want Jesus and the way to get to Him is by traversing the path He has marked out for us. We must expect it to include some difficulties. We must expect to feel some repugnance. But if God is asking us for something, we need to do it, and the sooner the better. The longer we moan and groan, the longer we suffer, really. The true apostle will serve. He knows no other way.

Be sure, of course, through discernment and direction that you are in fact being asked for this thing. We have all seen souls who torment themselves over matters that God does not want from them, thereby ignoring the obvious requests God is making such as kindness, patience, and love for those around us. This is another trap and I have discussed it in the past. It is by serving in remedial matters, in our vocations, that we are prepared to serve in heroic matters. If we master the building blocks to holiness, we will step up with confidence when the moment comes and we are asked to put ourself on the line for Jesus, as He put Himself on the line for us.

I hope I am clear. If we are in the habit of serving in small things, we will serve in big things. The more at stake, the more repugnance we may feel. Again, if your answer is "yes" to Jesus, your answer is "yes" to Jesus. Get on with His will once you discern it and do not keep the Lord and Master waiting.

When a soul is drifting out in nowhere land, that soul is easily distracted. The winds of the world blow freely out there, leaving a soul vulnerable to being whipped around from place to place. If this describes us, we will see that we lose interest in projects quickly and our positions on moral issues change from day to day. There is no anchor, you see, so any burst of change in the world can relocate us to somewhere else.

Clearly, this is no place for an apostle. It is uncomfortable to be on a path that is always shifting. The feet feel unsteady and this feeling of unsteadiness communicates itself to others through us, leaving them unsettled. One has only to look around to see what the impact of this unsteadiness has been on families and vocations.

Consider the family. If a mother is not rooted firmly on the side of the divine will, she will be easily called away from her husband and children by the world. This is how. As the winds in the world shift, a new wind proclaims that women are misused and unappreciated if they serve in the home. The mother who is out drifting in nowhere land can be influenced to bitterness. The enemy encourages this, whispering that the mother is being ill-used by her husband and children. Her mountain path, which includes beautiful service to these souls, is abandoned as this mother moves closer to the worldly side in search of the happiness that has now become elusive. She finds additional discontentment, of course, and her husband and children become unhappy and also discontented.

This is the very same with husbands and can be easily fitted to clergy also. Some clergy spend too much time in the world, with worldly souls. They begin to feel restless and instead of correctly identifying that they are spending too much time in the world and fleeing back into their vocations, they blame the vocation itself, incorrectly identifying their commitment to Christ as the source of the problem. Many have abandoned their vocations, seeking contentment in the world.

The point is that if a soul is not rooted in the divine will the soul is subject to being blown around and away from the mountain of holiness. When this occurs, many others are affected because each life involves other souls intended to benefit from that life. This situation is what Jesus is attempting to remedy through the renewal. We all have a role to play in this renewal and that role is clearly marked out in our vocation.

I worked in the pro-life movement before my marriage. After my marriage I continued this work. During a pregnancy, our group became involved in a situation where hostility from the other side erupted, creating low-level violence. My husband objected to my involvement from that time, citing the pregnancy as a reason why I should not be involved in direct protesting. I disagreed completely and said so. Upon discernment though, it was clear that my husband's concern for our unborn child had to be respected and that Jesus could not possibly want me to continue that work if it created discord in the family. I stopped and participated in other ways. My husband was well within his right to object and peace was restored in our home. My vocation had to take priority even over what I saw was God's work. It still does.

If we are looking for the anchor base, we usually need look no further than our vocations.

Unity with Jesus

When one considers that the soul is united to Jesus always, that Christ is omnipresent, then that soul will live differently. Let us stop what we are doing right now and acknowledge the presence of Jesus Christ. He is with us in each moment in time. If we grasp the barest understanding of this fact, we will alter our words, our actions, and our response to others. Given this, perhaps we should spend the smallest bit of time in our day welcoming Our Lord into our lives, often reminding Him of our love for Him and our need for Him. If we learn to live this truth, the world will change.

We must walk with this thought and I will show you how. Jesus asked me to record for Him one day. He said, *"I am with you."*

I said, "Yes, Lord, You are with me."

He said, *"I am with you, Anne."*

I said, "Of course, Lord, You are with me."

He said, *"Anne, you do not understand. For this day, carry your notebook with you as I want you to record for Me at a moment's notice. I have to help you to understand that I am with you."*

Well, this seemed inconvenient but my policy is to answer "yes" to Him so I put a little notebook in my pocket and marched into my day. My first port of call, as always, was the kitchen. My four year old was ill and had to miss pre-school. This did not sit well with her.

She said, "Mom, I want to go to school."

I said, "You can't go to school. You are sick."

She said, "Mom, please. We are painting today."

I looked at her poor little face, flushed and earnest, and

said gently, "You can't go to school, honey. You have a bug."

She frowned and said reproachfully, "Mom, I'm not a bug."

I laughed aloud and in my soul, Jesus also laughed.

His voice came, strong and true. He said, *"I am with you."*

Later, I went to get a haircut. It was far shorter than I had anticipated. This has happened to all of us. I left and got into the car. I said to myself in dismay, "It's too short."

Jesus said, *"Yes, but it won't interfere with your ability to work, so serve."*

I burst out laughing and Jesus said, *"I am with you."*

Still later, I looked at a card on the counter. My husband had left it out for me to sign. I have to say that I would not have been enthralled by the intended recipient and thought regretfully that this was a bad attitude. Overcoming myself, I did sign my name, and added a note inviting the recipient to come and stay with us.

Jesus spoke with great affection saying, *"Well done, Anne."*

And then, *"I am with you."*

At that moment, I got it. I really did. Jesus was with me. He was in the kitchen, He was in the car, and He was with me in all that I did for my children. I have lived differently since then because I am aware of His loving presence. Am I aware of His loving presence because He manifests Himself to me constantly? Not at all. I am aware of His loving presence because I believe in Him and I know Him through what the Bible tells me.

Everything I have ever read in the Bible has been borne out in my work for Christ and even though He often hides from me and challenges my faith, I live my decision to believe in Him. He is with us.

Let us, as lay apostles, look at our days through the eyes of Christ. We will take His presence into each conversation, each situation. We will adjust our goals for others and ourselves, always taking heaven's goals into account. Dear apostles, quite often, where the world sees failure, heaven sees success. Our yardstick for measuring just about everything changes when we begin to accept this and insert heavenly goals in place of earthly goals. Truly, He is with us.

We state again, God is with us. The Bible tells us this repeatedly. Jesus Himself says He will be with us, even until the end of time. We need no further proof. So today, and every day, we begin to live accordingly. If we try to do this, we will find that our transition from earth to heaven is a seamless one. We will blend gently from this world to the next and the presence of Christ will remain constant throughout.

My friends, I want to share the reason why I am so certain of this. During my experience of heaven, it was clear to me that Jesus was with me in a profound way. From the beginning of those experiences, what struck me most powerfully about heaven was that Jesus never left me. Initially, I accepted this in great joy and exulted in it, resting in it. After the first few experiences, I began to recover myself as it were and take notice of my surroundings. Did I see Jesus? If so, what did He look like? I could not in honesty say that I saw Him. The experience of Jesus was not visual. I experienced Him completely because He was within me. I was experiencing unity with Him.

As each experience was completed, I gently came to myself. During one of the latter experiences, I came to myself as Jesus was talking. My eyes opened and I became aware of the room and He continued to talk. This felt perfectly natu-

ral. When Jesus finished speaking, I nodded, understanding
His request. Suddenly, I was struck with something, once
again, but in a more complete way.

Jesus was with me. Jesus never left me. He never had. He
never would. Jesus had allowed me to experience Him profoundly during the heaven experience, and by remaining in
constant communication throughout the transition He illu-
minated His constant presence in each of us. I sat down at
my computer reverently, understanding more clearly than I
ever have that Jesus was with me.

Dear apostles, in the very same way, Jesus is with each of
us. Truly, the Kingdom of God is within us because Jesus IS
the Kingdom of God. I state clearly that in heaven, nobody
reacts when Jesus enters an area. Some souls smiled at me or
acknowledged me in welcome, but they did not acknowledge
Jesus. I found this odd until I understood that Jesus never
leaves any of these souls. The same way I experienced Him,
they experienced Him. This is the sublime truth that can
create peace in every soul.

There is no restlessness, no hungering, no longing, no fear,
no anxiety, and no disturbance possible when you are united
to Jesus. And He is with you. On earth, we must believe this
in faith. This is the treasure without price. Many souls on
earth search frantically, looking for this state of mystical paradise. But, like Dorothy wearing the red shoes in the *Wizard
of Oz*, this mystical state is with them all along and their
search is doomed at its inception unless the soul looks
within.

If we begin our climb up the mountain of holiness each
day, we will be accepting that Christ is within us. At the top
of this mountain is unity with Jesus, yes, and that unity is a
guaranteed thing if we desire it.

The higher we climb, the more we labor for holiness and

for the kingdom on the path that He has marked out for us, and the more we honor Jesus within our souls. Truly, the lay apostle has been given assurance that if that apostle works for Jesus, Jesus will care for all of his needs, including the conversion of the apostle's family. We need no further encouragement or promise. The only peace is found with Jesus. Paradise is a place. Heaven is vibrant with activity and joy and we will all get there. Work for Jesus, my friends, and we will bring as many souls home to our Father as we possibly can.

Faith

Lay apostles must allow their decision to serve Jesus to direct their days. Faith is a gift, after all, which ebbs and flows, comes and goes. On days when faith is weak, we must not throw our hands up in despair and abandon our missions. We must simply understand that Jesus is asking us to serve that day in darkness. Our merit will be based on our service and our love, not on our feelings. If we are serving on a day without feeling any faith, it simply means we are carrying a little something extra in our backpacks for heaven. We will see this at the end of our days.

We will always be happy we served Jesus, and for Jesus, others. This is not something that will cause us regret. What we will regret is a lack of service or a piecemeal kind of service that came and went with our feelings. Rise, serve, and love. Jesus will send courage and all of the faith that is necessary.

We must try for joy in service, joy in suffering, and even joy in doubt. The most beautiful perfect storm of suffering combines all three. Imagine the beauty of such a jewel when viewed from heaven.

So, dear apostles, be brave and serve. You are part of a heavenly team that cannot lose.

Part Four

Heaven Speaks

A Collection of Messages to
Specific Groups of Souls

Heaven Speaks About Abortion

Jesus

August 1, 2005

"My children, you are all so precious to Me. There is a temptation for souls to believe that if they have made a grave mistake, they are not welcome in heaven or that they are not suitable companionship for Me. This is not true. And this temptation must be fought against. Sin is forgivable. All sin. I want to direct attention here specifically to the sin of abortion. This sin has become so commonplace in your world that some souls have come to believe it is not serious. Well, dear little soul, you must understand that it is the enemy of all things living who has spread this error. This is a trick, a master deceit of such proportion that it has resulted in the slaughter of many. Now, you may wonder at My feelings on this. I will share them with you. I am grieved, in the extreme. I am sad each time I welcome a rejected little one back to Myself. And they are welcomed home, believe Me. I am all mercy and love and these little ones are in no way at fault, so heaven gives them great joy upon their return. In the same way, we will welcome you home, regardless of your sins. Be at peace. There are many souls in heaven who have committed sins of this magnitude. You might say heaven is filled

with sinners, My friend, but these are repentant sinners. Would you like to repent and serve as My beloved apostle? I know that you would and it is for this reason that I have come to you with these words. You are forgiven. I have many things to share with you that will help you to understand your situation. Rest your wounded little heart against Me now as I show you how to return in completeness."

St. Mary Magdalene

"I send the most loving greetings to my friends on earth. I am delighted that Jesus allows me to speak at this time. There are great things happening in the world and the renewal makes its way bravely from heaven to earth and from soul to soul. We are watching and helping from heaven. One of the signs that the renewal is necessary is the number of abortions that are occurring. My dear sisters in Christ, this is an abomination. We cannot allow it to continue, neither you nor I. We have to help our sisters to understand that there is a little life nestled in their womb, a life sent by God Himself. To think any differently is to become a plaything of the devil. There must be no discussion about this point in the sense that you must never allow yourself to consider, even for a moment, that a pregnancy does not equal a life, a person, a divine plan. Do not back away from this fact, this irrefutable truth. I want to speak to women who have had abortions and allowed their children to be taken from them in this way. Dear woman, if you think you have committed

a graver sin than I, you are wrong. Jesus loves me tenderly and I am a close friend to the Savior. And yet I would repel you if you knew how I had lived a part of my life. We are all the same in that we are all sinners. Nobody in heaven looks at anyone else with anything but love and understanding. This is because we all understand that given the right set of earthly circumstances, we could make grave mistakes such as you did. Your circumstances contributed to your decision. I know this. Jesus knows this. All of heaven knows this. You must accept this too. If you were in different circumstances, it is likely you would have made a different decision. But it is over and Jesus makes all things new. Let Him make your soul new and you will give Him far greater joy than you gave Him sorrow. I would not tell you something if it were not true. If you return to Jesus with your heart and ask Him for forgiveness, you will have forgiveness and He will forget your sins. He has certainly forgotten mine."

"My sisters in Christ, allow me, please, to help you. When you are caught in a web of guilt, it can be difficult to get out. It is actually impossible alone. The problem is that you can think so badly of yourself for your mistake that you begin to lose sight of your dignity and heavenly value. Jesus needs your help and you have to respond to Him. You know this. But before you can respond to Jesus you must allow Him to heal you. So put your hand out and Jesus will give a mighty pull. He will release you from the grip of pain that has held you captive. Jesus looks into your soul and He sees everything. He understands. You will face Him someday. It is inevitable. So face Him today and look closely. All you will see in His beautiful face is love. Jesus does not condemn you. It is the enemy telling you these things. Jesus is all mercy, all understanding. Let Him take your pain and replace it with

heavenly joy. Dear sister, do you think for a moment that the darkness of sin in the world has not claimed others in this way? You know that many have fallen victim to the falseness and the distortions of truth. You are not alone, by any means. Many women work hard for the kingdom and give Jesus great glory. They, also, have allowed their children to be taken in this way. But they returned to Christ in sorrow and He forgave them. He offers this to you now. We will surround you with heavenly grace and then you too will work for Jesus and for others. You will give great comfort and joy to these children of yours in heaven if you return to the family of God. There is nothing that should stop you. Come back to the heavenly side where you are cherished and, may I say, so badly needed."

August 2, 2005

"Dearest sister in Christ, this is the time to heal. Jesus is sending this period for all souls to return to His Sacred Heart. His healing graces are never-ending. There is enough for every bit of spiritual and emotional healing that is necessary for every soul who has ever been injured in any way. I am urging you to take advantage of this now so that you can return fully to the family of God and work for your brothers and sisters who remain in darkness and loneliness. So many are unloved. If you spend this period of time working for other souls in your life, wherever Jesus has placed you, there will be joy in heaven. You will give glory to Jesus and to your children who have come before you. They will be proud that you are their mother because you serve them on earth by serving Jesus. Do you believe me, my sister? I speak the truth. We in heaven never exaggerate and we never tell untruths. We speak carefully and our words are backed by

God Himself. Your children love you and have complete understanding of the fears that moved you to your decision. You will see them and you will spend eternity with them. There is only joy in heaven. Surely you understand that there will be no recriminations and you will have no grief in this divine land. You will be reunited with all of your loved ones and together you will explore the kingdom of the triumphant souls, who have conquered the world and their humanity. So there is no reason for you not to be joyful and peaceful. Jesus loves you. All the saints love you. The angels work tirelessly for your return to complete joy. And your children wait to be united to their mother."

"Sisters, I thank God for you. Your kindness to other women will bring more souls home to heaven. I never judged another woman after my conversion because I understood why a woman would make the choices that she made. Some choices are wrong. We all know that. Who can say that all choices are the correct choices? Here in heaven, we look at events in the world. I, in particular, see women who are assaulted sexually. I am familiar with the emotions that can erupt in a woman after such a thing occurs, either in childhood or in adulthood. These emotions, if not brought to heaven for healing, can result in bad choices. Perhaps you understand what I am referring to. Our bodies are intended for the most beautiful service to the kingdom. The sexual relationship between a man and a woman is holy and right when it is blessed by God. The sexual relationship between a man and a woman is neither holy nor right when it is not blessed by God. And when someone is used as an object for sin, all of heaven is disappointed. You are God's cherished woman. Do not allow your body to be misused. If this occurs against your will, you must be certain to talk to others who

have been misused in this way. Seek out others who are holy and who have healed. They will help you to understand that your sexuality is not something that can be taken from you by force. Also, your sexuality is not something that is impacted by being raped because you did not give freely. What I am saying to you is that your sexuality is intact and as beautiful as God created it. Also, if you have fallen victim to the modern deception that sinful physical intimacy is acceptable, you are not alone. Many holy souls have also made these mistakes. But here is God's promise to you. Confess your sins. Pour them all out where they cannot hurt you and He, Jesus, will take them away. They will be cast into the fires of His Sacred Heart and they will be incinerated and gone forever. Jesus will grant you complete healing. Be patient and let Him do this for you. Your purity will be returned to you and your beautiful sexuality will be restored to its original state. Remember that I told you that heaven speaks with great authority? Well, you can be assured that this promise comes from the throne of God. Walk in joy, dear sister of mine, because Jesus loves you."

Blessed Mother

"My dear little daughter, how I love you and wait to hold you in my arms. I watch you so carefully, alert to any opportunity to bring you to Jesus. I have seen every pain that you have suffered. I have witnessed each bitter tear. You will be fine now if you let us heal you. I want to take you by your hand and bring you to my Son. I will tell Him that I am proud of you because you

are courageous in admitting your mistakes and asking
for forgiveness. Can you imagine the smile Jesus will
have for you? He is so beautiful and His eyes will fill
with love for you. You see, Jesus does not care what you
have done. He does not sit and think constantly about
your mistakes. He thinks constantly about your heart
and its brokenness. He thinks constantly about His
need to have you safe in the family of Christ. He considers all of the good that you are capable of bringing
to other souls. Jesus needs you. I, your heavenly
mother, need you. Will you help us? Come to your
mother now and rest your head against me. You do not
see me but I promise you that I am with you. I will
never leave you. I have brought many women back to
Jesus and they give Him the greatest love and fidelity.
That is how I can see you, my daughter. I see you as a
loyal, loving servant of Jesus, who desires to place constant healing graces into your soul."

Heaven Speaks About Addictions

Jesus

July 27, 2005

"My dear soul, you are chosen to serve in the kingdom of God. Nothing can refute this statement. I am Jesus and I need you to help Me. There is a temptation to believe that you will have many days in which to serve heaven. Because of this temptation, souls feel they can languish at times, certain that while they do not serve completely today they will do so tomorrow. Well, tomorrow is not what I am calling you to. I am calling you into this day, today. This is the time to let go of any habit that is pulling you away from Me and pulling you away from service to Me. Dear apostle, you must give Me your addiction. It can never be a good thing to be overly attached to something that dulls your ability to love. Look into your soul right now. You will find that I am looking back at you. You know that I am asking you to put aside this addiction. You have known this for some time. The day is today. I am not looking for service tomorrow. You may never see tomorrow because that is how life on earth is designed. Man never knows when he will be called home to heaven. There is a part of you that is fearful. You fear that you cannot be happy without this addiction.

Will you believe Me when I tell you that it is quite the opposite? You cannot be happy with the addiction because it is numbing you from experiencing Me. I am in other people. I am in your loved ones. But you are putting this addiction in a place above Me and consequently above your loved ones, as well as others. Dearest apostle, I will take this addiction from you. I will do this for you if you let Me. But you have to be willing to accept My grace in your soul. I will do all of the difficult work, the work that you fear. You will remain in the present, in each moment, and you will have grace enough to walk away from this dependence. That is My promise."

St. Barnabas

August 1, 2005

"My dear friend, notice that Jesus calls you His apostle. He is asking you to serve Him. Do not make the mistake of thinking that He is talking to someone else. He is talking to you. There is work for you in the kingdom. You have suffered, it is true. We all suffer during our time on earth. But Jesus can heal any wounds. You are trying to heal yourself. You are trying to make yourself feel better. But you cannot do this alone and the healing you are offering your body and soul is making you sicker. I have the true healing, the true peace. I am Barnabas and I want to help you too. It can be difficult to make a decision to step away from your addictions. I

understand. *The enemy convinces you that you need these things to be happy. And yet, you are not happy. Be honest with yourself for a moment and hear me. You are not at peace if you are attached to something so much that you need it, unless it is God. I am referring generally to things that you are putting in your body, but any habit can become destructive if it takes you from your duties or separates you from purity or holiness. Some of these things are fine in moderation, perhaps, but in excess they begin to take over. These things, these addictions, once they hold you, do not let you go until you make a firm decision to stop completely. Only then can heaven remove their power over you and free your soul. My friend, you object in your heart. You hold this addiction close to you and would like me to be wrong. This alone tells you that there is a problem. I am not wrong. I am looking from the heavenly perspective and I assure you, I am correct when I tell you that Jesus wants to free you."*

"Jesus wants you to view the world as He views the world. Only in this way will you serve Him as He needs you to serve. Only in this way will you see those around you with His eyes and correctly identify your role in their lives. If you have an addiction, you have acquired a bad thing, and that is tunnel vision. You see with the eyes of your addiction. You will serve, yes, but only in as much as it does not interfere with your addiction. Do you understand? The addiction begins to take the first place in your life, putting Jesus and your vocation in the second. This tunnel vision gradually closes off the heavenly vision until, at the end, when the addiction rules you, you can see only it. You are then the servant to the addiction. The addiction is your master. And the addiction is not a benign master, seeking your welfare. The addiction is a cruel master eventually demanding everything

from you. You will have to bring the addiction offerings of your dignity, your purity of intention, and perhaps even your membership in the Body of Christ. Now, you say I am exaggerating. You cannot fool me because I know what you are thinking. I am one who understands addiction, having suffered from it myself. You are not unique when you suffer from an addiction. We end up the same way. Compare the master that is your addiction to Jesus Christ. Jesus seeks only your welfare and the welfare of those around you. He asks you to serve in dignity, in goodness, in company with all of the just on earth and the saints in heaven. You are surrounded by heavenly beings in the form of angels who will assist you in each moment and in every situation. Jesus sends you His Spirit, who enlightens you and gives you courage and strength. Jesus has prepared a place for you here in heaven. I can go to this place and see it because it is here. We do not tell lies. We deal only in the truth. I would like you to sit silently before Christ now in this Spirit of truth and let Jesus tell you if your addiction is a problem."

"I want to tell you about the price you are paying to maintain this addiction as your friend. And that is how you view it, is it not? You think this addiction is a good thing for you, a consolation, and a compensation for the pain you have suffered. Let me state again, lest you have forgotten. Pain is a universal experience. Hurt is a universal experience. You are not alone in your pain and in your hurt. Do not think you are somehow entitled to this addiction because you have suffered more than others. This would be false, a lie, and remember that heaven does not deal in lies. So where there is only truth, we must speak with clarity. Everyone on earth has been hurt or will be hurt and has felt pain or will feel pain. That makes you like everyone else. You are not entitled

to use this addiction to dull your pain. It is wrong, a sin. To say that you are in special need of this earthly balm is making an excuse. It is also preventing you from dealing with your pain. And what happens when people do not deal directly with their pain? The enemy turns the pain to bitterness. In souls who allow Jesus to help, pain becomes wisdom and compassion. Pain is used for great spiritual growth. Do not listen to those who tell you that your addiction is acceptable because you suffer. These people are leading you away from Christ through flawed thinking. This is the thinking that leads souls to hell. I am not saying that you are going to hell. I am not saying that those who have died in their addictions are in hell. Jesus is all mercy. He is all goodness and forgiveness. He does not condemn a soul unless a soul insists on being condemned. But it is because of His very goodness and mercy that you should serve Him more completely and you cannot do that if you serve another master."

July 29, 2005

"Be at peace in this struggle, understanding that you do not struggle alone. It is wise to know when you need help. This project, freeing yourself from an addiction, is not something you should try to do without heavenly help. There are many great saints who suffered from the difficulties you are experiencing. These souls, men and women of good will, fought against their selfish desires and replaced their will with His will. This is what you are being asked to do. We, the saints in heaven, are all going to pray that Jesus will send you the greatest heavenly assistance. You will be surrounded by grace, which is heaven's power. When you feel you are struggling you must cry out to heaven for more graces and we will obtain them for you immediately. You see, Jesus needs your *help. He needs your service. You cannot serve Him as you would like, or as He needs you to serve, when you are carrying the weight from this addiction. If Jesus frees you from this addiction, you will become a great apostle. Your role in the kingdom will become clear to you and you will use this clarity to illuminate others. Think back on your life to those who have helped you through difficulties. These souls were serving heaven. You must do the same. There are many souls whom you are destined to assist. You do not want to reach the end of your life and find that these souls went without necessary assistance because you were trying to numb yourself. Dear friend, be at peace. You are being called by name. Answer 'yes' to Jesus and He will take care of all of your difficulties.*

St. Clare of Assisi

"My dearest friends on earth, how happy I am to speak with you. I am Clare and I want to encourage you to take the first step. The first step you must take to become free of an addiction is this. Raise your eyes to Jesus Christ and say, 'Lord, help me, for I cannot do this alone.' How Jesus delights in this prayer. How His heart leaps with joy that one of His own has acknowledged both His power and His love. You see, my dear friend, when you cry out in this way you are trusting in His love for you, as well as in His mercy. You are saying, 'Yes, Lord, I have made mistakes, but I know Your love for me is intact.' Even if it is only the smallest part of you that dares to hope Jesus will help you, that is enough. Jesus needs nearly nothing to flood mercy down upon a soul. Even if you have committed the most vile and constant sins, even if you

*feel that you are the most despised creature in the universe,
you must cry out to Him. The truth is that He loves you. He
is waiting for you and watches closely for your smallest opening to Him. Won't you try this, my friend? You have tried to
make yourself feel better in other ways and you have been left
in despair. Now try Jesus. I am praying for you right now,
that you will allow the door of your soul to open, even the
smallest bit. If you do this, the light will flood in. Be humble,
admit you have committed sins, and ask for forgiveness. You
will not be disappointed. Jesus will claim you as His own and
restore you to the dignity that rightfully belongs to a child of
God."*

St. Andrew

*"My friends on earth, you are often willing to admit that
your life is not going as well as you would like or as well as
you had hoped. This series is designed to provide you with
the grace to understand why this is the case. Whatever your
problems or crosses, addictions make them worse. What happens is this. You are given a certain number of crosses to
carry. This is the way it is set up. Only in heaven will you be
free of all suffering. It is through these struggles that you earn
your salvation. So your suffering is of heavenly design and
purpose. But a soul who is in the grip of an addiction has
added so much weight to his cross that often he cannot carry
it. Souls then blame the cross, stating that Jesus has made it
too difficult. This is false. The soul himself, through his constant saying 'yes' to this addiction, has added unmanageable
weight to his life and to his cross. The soul uses the added*

weight to justify the addiction. 'I use this addiction because I carry such an unusual and painful cross.' This reasoning is distorted. Dear apostle, this will not work for you. It is not working for you now. When you are free of the addiction we can help you to shift the burden of whatever cross you are carrying so that it becomes a manageable thing for you. This is how God intended it to be. He does not load down His children with sorrow that cannot be managed. If you are suffering, we will help you. If you are bitter, Jesus will heal you. These are promises. We do not speak like some souls on earth. When we speak, we mean what we say and our promises are solid. They do not shift from one day to the next. You will have our help, but you must give heaven the addiction. Hand it to Jesus and He will take it from your hands, leaving you with all of heaven's help and a life that is manageable for you."

Blessed Mother

"Hello, my little children. I am Mary, your heavenly mother. I am with you in every suffering and I wait for an opportunity to assist you. Let me help you now in this struggle. I have helped many to overcome these earthly attachments and serve my Son more fully. I can do this for you too. You must realize that in heaven you will find no recriminations. We do not judge you for your sins. We simply ask you to step away from them. Jesus will cleanse your soul and you will have peace and joy as you learn again how to give His love to others. Too many of heaven's children are living in loneliness and pain. I cannot bear it, my child. This is not the way you are asked to live on earth. The sadness of my children is a painful cross for me. I beg God without pause for each one of you. I am begging Him right now for you, my little beloved soul. I am asking Him to give you exceptional grace to see your addiction as a block to heaven's light. Push it away from you, little dove, and Jesus will be on the other side, doing all of the work. It is only in the very beginning that it seems like a mountain and that is because you are counting on yourself. That is a mistake. Never rely on yourself to do something that heaven wants to do for you. Put your hand in your mother's now and I will lead you away from the addiction."

Heaven Speaks to Victims of Clerical Abuse

Jesus

August 13, 2005

"I send the greatest graces of healing for souls who have been misused by those claiming to work for My Church. Dearest souls of the kingdom, you must understand that such abuse was never willed by Me. I, your Jesus, can only will what is good. In this Age of Disobedience, many souls have departed from My will. They follow their own will and seek their own interests. Your suffering is the result of such self-will. Heaven views everything. I do not turn away from even the basest, most evil sin, because I must witness all that occurs on the earth in order to judge in all justice. I am aware of what happened to you. Those responsible will face Me and there will be no hiding, I assure you. My justice will be complete. I am speaking now, not to those who committed these crimes. They must repent and their repentance is a separate issue. Souls guilty of such acts must seek absolution in the Sacrament of Penance."

"Today I speak to the victims of such sin. Dear soul, I will heal you. I have your healing here and you have only to ask for it. I want your soul to be the most beautiful and pure soul possible.

There is so much that the kingdom of God needs from you. There are souls in pain whom you can help. I want only what is good for you. You have suffered at the hand of one who served the enemy. You can accept bitterness, yes, because this is your choice. Or you can come to Me, Jesus, and allow Me to heal your heart and soul and restore you to the dignity that belongs to you and that can never be taken by force. There are always those who commit sins such as these. But when a soul claims to serve heaven and exploits those around him for selfish purposes, the wounds go very deep. I know this. You were betrayed, dear soul, and what happened to you was also a betrayal of Me. I take both betrayals seriously. For this reason, I am allotting unlimited graces for your healing. Come to Me and let Me remove your pain. I will do this for you. And you will serve the kingdom in great joy, and together, you and I will have destroyed the bitter plan of the enemy."

St. John the Apostle

"Dear souls, I am so grateful to come to you today. I love Jesus so much that I have difficulty talking about it. I want to try though, because I want you to love Him also. Jesus is so good and kind. His heart is rarely moved to anger. Well before Jesus feels anger, He feels pity and compassion. He so understands humanity and the sufferings of humanity. The

situation on earth at this time, when certain servants of Christ have abused those around them, has caused Him to suffer and grieve. Jesus is kind, yes, but He is also moved to anger when humanity strikes out at each other in cruelty. And who can say that these attacks on innocence were not cruel? This is the worst that humanity has to offer and these sins will be punished. We do not talk about punishment often because God is so merciful and when souls repent, He forgives. But there is also the fact that sin can cause damage to others. My friends, the ones responsible for these attacks are not only responsible for the damage they have done to you, but for the damage they have done to the universal Church during a period in history when souls badly need to rely on their Church. This period is ending, through God's mercy, and the Church will be restored, but the damage will have to be recompensed. This is not your concern, of course. Your concern is Jesus Christ and your soul's relationship with Him. I am coming today to beseech you to allow Jesus to heal your wounds. Come back to Jesus and allow His grace to remove any bitterness you feel. Tell Jesus what is disturbing you and what you would like Him to remove and He will do this for you. When someone is injured by another, it is easy to feel great anger at the offender. I understand. I felt this myself when I lived on earth. Jesus showed me that the anger I was feeling damaged me more than any crime committed against me. In view of this, I had to make a decision to let go of the anger and consign the one who hurt me to God's justice. I walked away from the anger and left it with Jesus. I want you to do this too, so that you can be joyful again. There are souls reading these words who have already done this and they feel peace. I am glad. There are also those reading this who have not been able to recover. Ask Me, John, to help you. I have such influence with Jesus because I love Him so much. Jesus cannot refuse souls who love Him. This is good for you to know. Perhaps, though, you are angry at Jesus. Perhaps you blame Him for allowing this attack on you. My friend, my dear friend, Jesus did not do this. He did not assault you. You may say that Jesus allowed it, yes, and He has also allowed you to commit many sins. This is because Jesus has given you free will, the same way He gave the one who assaulted you free will. Jesus did not give your assailant free will so that he could assault you. He gave this person free will so that the soul could choose heaven freely. You have been given free will for the same reason, so that you can choose the kingdom of God. What will you choose? Will you choose darkness simply because someone else did? Of course not. You see the folly in that mistake. You would not want to hurt someone else as you were hurt. Let me help you to move away from this."

"When you come to heaven, you will understand everything. Heaven is a joyful place, filled with happiness. There is only love here. I want to explain something to you about the souls here. They all experienced some kind of pain when they lived on earth. The experience of being in exile, in humanity, insures that some pain will be felt. Suffering comes in so many ways that it would be tedious to list them. But your suffering will not make you stand out here in heaven. You will fit right in. There is something else I should remark about the souls here. They all forgave someone for something. Often it is hardest to forgive injury committed against someone you love. When your loved one is hurt, you can be in the same situation as the victim, only worse. Often the victim will move past the pain and forgive, but loved ones continue to suffer. This compounds the problem. The darkness then spreads further. One thing is for certain, my

friends. You will forgive before you come to heaven. You would not want to be here and be angry because you would be uncomfortable. I know that some are thinking that it will be impossible to forgive the wrongs that have been committed against them. And you may be right. For you to obtain this forgiveness alone is impossible. But all is possible for Jesus. He can do anything. Ask Jesus to place this forgiveness in your heart so that you can be healed and move on to all that is good and holy. Tell Jesus that you are afraid to ask for forgiveness. Perhaps you really are not sure that you want this gift. You see, if you hold on to your anger, you have a reason to be unhappy and that means you do not have to change. Change can make people fearful. But it is time to change now. I am John and I love you. I can see your struggles and I want to help you. It is for this reason that I am gently asking you to give this to Jesus. Let Jesus do all the work. He will take your anger, He will replace it with forgiveness, He will heal your heart, and you will learn to love Him like I love Him. And you will be happy. And I will be joyful. And when you come to heaven, I will be here waiting for you and I will congratulate you on making such a wise and brave decision."

"Dear soul, did you suspect that I would ask you to pray for the one who hurt you? You knew that I would, I am sure. There are some who are doing this. Well done. You understand, perhaps, God's wrath, and you correctly wish to deflect it from anyone. There are some who sigh greatly and say, 'My goodness, this John asks a lot.' I do, my friend, it is true. But I do not ask for myself but for you and the good of your soul. And I ask for Jesus too, because I see His pain at your distress. Jesus wants you back in His Sacred Heart where He can nurture and protect you. Another very impor-

tant reason I am seeking you out is because of the good you are destined to do for the kingdom of God. We need your service, dear apostle. You cannot be out of commission during this time because you are important and we need all souls on earth working for God. There is nothing as joyful for heaven as a soul who has been hurt, who forgives, and who then seeks to assist others. This gives the greatest meaning and benefit to your suffering and completely negates the damage the enemy wished to spread. It is like you are saying, 'No. I reject darkness and it will not be spread through me.' This thrills us, the saints, because this is what we did and it is for this reason we are saints. You are being called to be a saint, too. Say 'yes' to Jesus He will heal you and you will begin to work for heaven."

"Jesus brings good from bad. He is the master of bringing good from bad. You may not be able to imagine how Jesus could bring good from what happened to you but I promise you, He will find a way. Trust Him to do this. Rise each morning, give Jesus your day, tell Him that you trust Him, and watch the good He will bring through you. Dear soul, you have a great deal to offer heaven. Be deeply peaceful during this time and allow Jesus to quietly, gradually, heal you and make you holy. Be open to His love and to the love of others, as best you can. Jesus will do the rest. You will begin to know joy again. You want this, I know. There are souls who have been walking in darkness and they are weary. If you are one of these souls, give Jesus your hand and He will give a mighty pull. With all heavenly power, Jesus will wrest your soul from darkness and pull it into the light. Perhaps you are concerned that you have also sinned. Perhaps, in your pain, you began to walk a path that does not lead to Jesus or to heaven or to holiness. Perhaps you are fearful that

given your own sins, Jesus will not want you to work for the kingdom. Remember how I told you that heaven is filled with souls who have been hurt? It is true. But these same souls who fill heaven have also sinned. Our Lady often comforts souls this way. Heaven is filled with repentant sinners. If you repent, you will fit right in with us in that way also. None of us judges. We leave that for Jesus. You do the same. Confess your sins and step away from the patterns that are hurting you. Come back to Jesus now in all trust. You are welcomed and cherished. Only good things will result in a decision for your God. Close your eyes and know that the forgiving eyes of Jesus Christ rest upon you. There is nothing to fear. He understands everything."

Blessed Mother

"My dear little children, I am with you. I am Mary, your heavenly mother. I see everything that has happened to you and my heart aches with your pain. For a mother to see a child injured in any way is dreadful. For a mother to see the trust and innocence of her child betrayed is almost unendurable. And yet I have had to endure this, not only during this time, but also in the past. The consolation I rest in is the ability of my Son to heal and reward. He heals injured souls and restores them to purity. He then rewards them with unimaginable generosity for the goodness they allow to flow through them into the world. This consoles me. Just as I see your pain at the betrayal you experienced, I watched my Son's pain at the betrayal He experienced.

Such benefits came from the Passion of Jesus. We are all reaping the benefits. My dearest little child, will you place your hand in mine and let me help you? If you do this, I will be certain that you get to Jesus and remain with Him. He will heal you. And then the world will benefit from your suffering because Jesus will flow the greatest rewards through you for your decision to forgive. You can obtain healing graces for your soul, but also for all the souls around you. Ask Jesus to grant graces for your loved ones. He will do this. And you will understand that Jesus can turn your pain to joy. I am your mother and I love you most tenderly. I will help you in everything."

Heaven Speaks to Consecrated Souls

Jesus

August 12, 2005

"I speak today to all souls who have vocations in the Church. Dear souls consecrated to Me, I rely on you more than you understand. At this time I intend to use you powerfully to witness to heaven's presence on the earth. The period of time that is ending, the Age of Disobedience, has taken many of My consecrated souls from Me, and they live out their lives away from their vocations. They are forgiven, of course, and cherished, and many serve Me beautifully in other ways. I do not waste the presence of a willing soul, as you all know. If a soul loves Me I will find work for that soul and begin to prepare the soul's reward. I consider each one of you a heavenly asset. You have faced many challenges, it is true, and to have held your course steadily through these years is an achievement. Now I am asking you to move even closer to My heart. I want you to draw your every breath for Me, My desires and My needs. If you do this, unite yourself completely to Me, every moment of your remaining time on earth will be utilized. I will draw graces from the time you rise to the time you retire and from even your rest. Give Me everything. Replace any remaining self-will with My holy will. Tell Me often that I own

*your vocation. How this consoles Me and comforts
Me. You see, I am suffering. I suffer from the
anguish of the souls on earth who wander in
darkness. I suffer from the rebellion that causes
such upset in families and even in My Church.
But you will help Me and this gives Me solace.
Work for Me, please, in everything you do. I will
not hide My will and that is My promise to you."*

St. Dominic

"My brothers and sisters are truly blessed to live in a time
such as this. Fidelity to Christ and to your vows is an opportunity for the greatest nobility that God can allow for those
on earth. Obedience. This word is like heavenly music. Obey
in everything. Pledge to yourself that you will set the most
constant example of obedience to souls in your life. If you do
this, you will stand out starkly against the current landscape.
God's followers always stand out so this will be a good thing
for you. You will not stand out in heaven. You will blend into
the landscape here and this also is a good thing, indeed the
best thing for you. I helped the Church through a difficult
time and you are being asked to do the same. Your God is
everything to you, of course. Be sure that this is the case and
if it is not, change your life until it becomes the case. You will
want to heed me in this, dear brothers and sisters, because
the regrets you will experience if you do not serve will be profound and will cause you the greatest distress. Do not seek
the world's approval. Leave that for those who do not follow
Jesus Christ. Seek only His approval and do so in the spirit of

obedience always. You may say that this is a simple lesson and you may wonder why I highlight this so strongly. Well, in an Age of Disobedience, when most disobey and rebel, it is up to God's chosen ones to be vigilant in illustrating a different way. Souls should view your vocation and your joy in your vocation and consider that peace comes from service to God. If you are disobedient to your Church, you will be accountable. This is also a strong statement. I understand and speak deliberately. Guard your tongue carefully in these times and do not allow the influence of others to pull you away from fidelity to your Church. You must influence others to be faithful. They should not influence you to be unfaithful, even in your heart."

"When you take a step toward purity God lavishes graces upon you. You must allow Jesus to purify your soul in order for Him to possess it. Servants of Christ, confess your sins. Always speak and think like Jesus. Our good and kind Jesus understands that you struggle and He does not see these struggles as a problem. They are part of your movement to unity. Do not fear the struggles. But you must struggle. Remove anything from your life that encourages impurity of thought or intention. You cannot live like others in the world. A problem for many religious today is that they are trying to live two ways and they experience conflict. They then incorrectly decide that it is their vocation causing the conflict. Well, if the vocation were being lived in purity there would be no conflict. Do you understand? Do not pull away from the vocation to seek your peace and contentment. Pull away from the world and move further into your vocation and you will find the peace that is justly yours. This is a common mistake for many religious today and you know that I speak the truth. This is why many have left their vocations. They could

not reconcile one, the world, with the other, their vocation. So they made the wrong choice. They chose the world, seeking peace. Most do not find peace in the world, but if they seek Jesus He rewards them and all is well. Most decisions to serve Jesus in a religious vocation, though, are sound decisions. Sacrifice is required, of course, and some find they are uncomfortable with the required sacrifices or they are unsuited for the life. In these cases, they serve Jesus in another way and this is acceptable to heaven. The desire to serve heaven is good and holy and comes from heaven. Embrace this call."

"Jesus must be the center of your day. You must begin each morning by offering Jesus your day. And then everything in your day can belong to Him and be blessed by Him. Each morning you must rededicate your life to Him. This does two things. It gives Jesus joy and it clarifies in your mind that you work for Him and only for Him. The self-will that permeates the world today has contaminated many vocations. We do not wish to do something or we find it repugnant so we simply do not do it. This was never the way to heaven and it is not the way to heaven now. You will often find God's will repugnant to you and you will often have to do battle with yourself to become comfortable in the service to which He is calling you. My friends in Christ, you know that this is the way to heaven. There is a need to overcome yourself. Expect this. If you work in the spirit of obedience to God's will and not your own, it will become easier and easier to overcome yourself and you will move closer and closer to the heart of your Savior. The closer you come to Him, the less you struggle with self-will. The closer you come to Him, the less you consider how the world is viewing you. The closer you come to Jesus, the more you will long for Him and seek only Him.

This is a good place to be when you are on earth because Jesus then flows through you without obstruction. That stated, the struggles you experience are willed by heaven so do not think that you are not called to great holiness because you struggle. Be content to be small in your spiritual life and Jesus will be big. Humility comes from an awareness of one's flaws and humility is a necessity in your vocation. God is great and you are willing. This is how you are to proceed."

"You are cherished. Every saint in heaven is grateful to you. Our beautiful Blessed Mother, Mary, watches over you carefully. Do not think that you can do without her help. She has the most merciful gaze you will ever encounter. Mary wants to help you to purify your vocation. She will help you to identify when you are seeking your will and when you are seeking Christ's will. I love her with a love that cannot be quantified. You will love her in the same way when you know her. I am asking you to trust me about this today. If you love her, you will not be sorry. Our Lady has only the choicest gifts and graces for you. She has been so maligned on earth and this grieves our Jesus terribly. Be one who defends this spotless heavenly mother. "Mary." Say her name throughout your day and she will nourish you as a mother nourishes an infant. I speak now as your brother, who wants only what is best for you. If you do not have a devotion to this woman, I am beseeching you to seek one. Only holiness and peace come from a relationship with Mary. Only blessings and purity come from her. Joy and peace flow out from her to all she encounters. Families and vocations are restored. If you are in any way struggling today, seek Mary's help. You will not be disappointed. If you are not struggling, be grateful to Mary because it is a given that she has helped you in the past. Jesus only blesses those who love His mother. Do not think you are

above a devotion to Our Lord's mother. Do not be superior to
those who love her. There would be only one fool in that case,
my friend. Mary is your mother. She will help you in everything. Begin to say the Rosary and be certain that you pray
like a small child. Pray with trust and devotion, with confidence and love. Pray in the presence of the Eucharistic Christ.
And then observe the changes in yourself. If you are already
praying the Rosary, you understand what I am speaking
about and you are nodding your head in agreement with
these words. Either way, I am with you and intercede on your
behalf. There are countless saints in heaven, and countless
angels, both on earth and in heaven, willing to defend and
protect your vocation. Do not think you are alone or that the
battle is yours to win or lose. You are part of a heavenly team
that has already won. The outcome of the battle is decided.
But you must continue to fight your fight for a time longer."

"My dearest beloved friends, one of the ways that darkness
is being spread is through the promotion of healing powers
that do not originate with Christ. These powers, limited of
course, originate with the enemy of Christ. Jesus is sending
unlimited graces for spiritual healing and conversion. He is
sending great peace to those who come to Him and to those
for whom you intercede during this period. I am asking you
to speak out against powers that are not from heaven. The
enemy would like to make the world think we live in a new
age but as I have said, we live not in a new age but an Age of
Disobedience. Souls do not seek Jesus because if they seek
Jesus they will have to obey. If you are looking to avoid service, you do not seek the one who requires your service. Do
you understand? Let us take the example of a fortune teller.
Why does a soul seek to have his fortune told? The holy path
leads to trusting Jesus with the future and relying on His

providence. The exercise of such patience and trust builds sanctity and unity with heaven. In this time though, the enemy lures souls to disobedience by saying that such things as fortune telling are simply amusing and harmless. I assure you, we in heaven are appalled and saddened, not only by such widespread acceptance of these sinful practices, but by the failure of many of God's servants to speak out strongly against them. If you are walking with Jesus in the way in which you are called to walk with Jesus, you will not miss an opportunity to correct those in error. Always identify the source of the alleged power. If it is not Jesus, it is not from heaven and it is not acceptable for God's children."

Blessed Mother

"How heaven delights in the souls who dedicate their lives on earth to the goals of God. You are our treasure, our gold. You have been given a role to play in this time and you will do so. Jesus depends on your 'yes,' little one, and I know you will not disappoint Him. I know that you will serve heaven and I want to help you. With heaven there is joy that is not replaceable by anything that comes from the world. Only heaven's followers have this joy. We want to spread this heavenly joy throughout the world at this time and you know that we want to do this through you. We will give you joy as a gift that you can share with others. Ask us and we will place it in your heart. Come to me often for any assistance you require. If your heart is heavy, rest in my Immaculate Heart and I will share your burdens.

In this way you will be lighter and heaven will flow through you more efficiently. Only rewards will come to you. Be pure in your vocation, please, and you will bring so many souls with you that you will be delighted. Each soul enhances the kingdom of God in a special way, so each soul is precious and important. Treat each day as a day filled with the possibility of bringing souls to Jesus, even if you never see another person all day. Your offering of your day to Jesus brings Him souls. How sweet is the service to heaven when your vision is aligned with His. I am with you and I will never leave you. The days will fly, my dearest child, and you will be home with us soon. Be at peace now and let Jesus use you completely."

Heaven Speaks About Depression

Jesus

August 8, 2005

"I send the greatest graces of courage to all who read these words. My children in the world can become discouraged and sad. Dearest little ones, if you are this way, you must come to Me and rest your worries in My heart. I do not like to see you sad, even though life can be difficult. You feel you are alone and that is part of the reason why you feel such sadness. But you are never alone because I never leave you. To leave you would be acting against My very nature and such a thing is impossible. I am with you now, as you read these words, and I minister to your wounded heart with graces of love and courage. Continue on and I will send you relief. I have told you this and you must believe Me. It would also be acting against My nature to tell an untruth so you may believe Me and trust Me when I say this to you. I will send you relief. Bring all of your sadness to Me. Pour it out to Me. I will listen and I will continue to listen for days and days and on into eternity if necessary. I have the time, My beloved apostle. I am not too busy to listen to you. You may cry if you wish because I assure you, when I lived upon the earth, I also cried. Pain is unavoidable until you

arrive in heaven. You are not the only one who suffers in this way. There are many souls in your world today who are suffering the sadness that you are feeling. Your world does not always nourish souls. Only I, the Divine Healer, can heal you. I can give you nourishment that will set your soul alight again. Come to Me in all trust. Be patient, while I see to your wounds and hurts. You did not become sad like this in a moment. Come to Me all throughout your day and allow Me to help you carry this heavy cross of sadness."

St. Dymphna

"My most loving greetings flow down to you. I am asking Jesus to send you a glimpse of heavenly joy. If you have this glimpse, even the smallest bit, you will proceed in great hope, because you will know that you will not feel this way forever. And that is your fear, is it not? That you will be sad and downhearted forever? I am going to ask you to look at things a little differently. If you do, I feel sure you will find strength. You are only on the earth for a short time. There are many souls on earth today who do not see with clarity. They, these poor mistaken souls, think that the world and the time spent on earth are all that matter. They think you are on the earth to have fun. Well, this is not the case. Jesus is joyful, of course. Apostles who are serving Jesus are joyful. But your life on earth is not playtime. It is time for service to heaven. Many beloved servants of Jesus suffer from great sadness and loneli-

ness. You might say that this condition is common. Let me explain it another way. While I was on the earth, I knew that I was separated from Jesus. I did not want to be separated from Jesus. This made my heart terribly heavy and sad. But I also knew that Jesus needed me to serve cheerfully, so this is what I did. I served as cheerfully as possible and allowed Jesus to use my sadness to console others. I traded my sadness for graces to heal others and bring others to His heart. This made me feel better because I knew that I was helping Jesus and working with heaven. It gave me a feeling of accomplishment, even in my depression. I am going to ask you to do the same thing. First, though, we will ask Jesus to heal you. It is always the right thing to do to ask for healing. If Jesus heals you, you will serve Him, of course. If Jesus wills that you carry the cross of sadness for a time longer, will you allow me, Dymphna, to assist you? I am going to obtain graces for you that will give you fresh strength. The kingdom needs you. Jesus needs you. We will work together, you and I, to insure that souls are benefiting from any sadness that is yours."

"*Dear soul, how you suffer because you do not feel understood. Others make your cross heavier through their judgments and impatience. I want to tell you that I understand. I understand completely. And more important than my understanding is the total understanding that comes from Jesus Christ. Jesus knows your every hurt. He loves you so tenderly and wants to help you. Do you allow Him into your pain? Do not keep this pain from Him because if you do, you make it worse. Constantly give Him your pain. There are few souls on earth who use heaven as completely as heaven would like to be used. Trust heaven for everything. You worry that you are not pleasing to heaven because of your sadness and heavy heart. I assure you, heaven is pleased right now that you are taking the time to read these words and work with us. You are not a burden to heaven. You are heaven's joy and you are a gift to the world in which you live. You may feel you are not treated like a gift in the world. That may be very true. But most of heaven's greatest gifts to the world are treated badly so do not let this worry you. Look what they did to our Jesus. The world does not always recognize heaven's little treasures. But you are different because you are going to trade earthly eyes for heavenly eyes. Look with the eyes of heaven now and view your suffering as temporary and valuable. Soft little hearts are wounded easily, but that does not mean you should desire to have a hard heart. I shudder at the thought. Be happy with the heart that Jesus has given you. Seek understanding from the angels and saints and you will find it. Be patient with those around you because perhaps they are in their own pain and it makes them unable to minister to you. This is the state in much of the world, my dear friend. That is why there is so much sadness. But we will deal with your sadness first, and then you will help others to find heaven's joy."*

"Do not be afraid. There is nothing that should make you be afraid. Jesus will care for your needs and you will care for His. Fear is paralyzing many on earth at this time. This brings us back to the need for the heavenly eyes. If you look at your situation and view it as heaven views it, you will understand that there is nothing on the earth that should make you fearful. You will serve for a time and then you will die in your body. This is the way it has always been. This is heaven's plan. This is not a bad thing but a good thing. Imagine living on earth indefinitely. That would make you sad because it would take away your hope that your time of service will end and your time in heaven will begin. If souls

on earth do not think well of you and they ridicule you, well, my friend, that puts you in the greatest company you could find. They did not think well of Jesus. They ridiculed Jesus. They put Him to death. He was the greatest gift of God, the gift of Himself, and they killed Him. Did this make Him any less a King? No. He is the King. So the treatment of the world does not dictate the treatment you will receive in heaven, where the first shall be last. Never fear the opinions of others on earth. Good and holy people understand your value and the value of your suffering. Step away from the opinions of others. Confess your sins. Let Jesus fill your soul and you will then reflect Jesus in the world, even in your suffering, or shall I say, especially in your suffering. As Jesus flowed through me, He will flow through you. All you have to do is agree to cooperate with Him. Offer Him each day in the spirit of love and patience. He will get you through another day, yes, which is another one of your fears, is it not? That you cannot get through a day? He will get you through that day and pre-serve each moment for eternity by using each moment for the salvation of others, who may be suffering even more than you. This is the truth. This is where you are needed at this moment perhaps. Will you make the most use of it?"

St. Paul

"My brothers and sisters suffering from sadness should take heart. The time for sadness is ending quickly. The dark-ness is lifting. Are these words not proof of that? You feel the great graces that flow from these words and from this mis-sion. Ask for these graces and continue asking for each soul

you meet because Jesus is not limiting the amount of love and healing He is sending during this time. Do you hear me? Jesus is not limiting graces. We should celebrate. You are thinking that perhaps St. Paul has gotten the wrong topic. How can I talk about joy when you feel so sad? Well, it is exactly then that I need to talk about joy and all of the saints will agree with me. You see, we had joy in hope but we did not always have joyful experiences on the earth. The very thought would make us shake our heads. We marvel sometimes at the depth of suffering that is possible while you are in exile, away from heaven. Our joy came in Christ and in the hope, well placed, that Jesus Christ lived and died and rose from the dead. Do not hope in earthly souls. They will let you down hard. They cannot help it. They have their own pains and struggles. Hope in Jesus only. If you do this, you will not be disappointed. So look at your sadness and say, 'Jesus, I carry this sadness for You. I look up at Your figure on the cross and I offer You my own anguish.' Together, you and Jesus will walk through your Calvary until He lifts it or He comes to take you home. You have a whole army of helpers in heaven who love you. We look at your struggle and we understand. Many of us carried that cross also. You are not alone. And you can be joyful because Jesus Christ lives and He will return to reclaim what is His. Now be brave a little while longer. Dymphna is right when she tells you to ask for healing. I, Paul, will join you and Dymphna in asking for your healing. We will all ask together. And if you receive healing, we will celebrate. And if you do not receive healing, we will celebrate, because all of God's will is good."

"Now, my friends, please understand that great sadness is not always a tragedy. If you never felt sad you would have difficulty in comforting others who feel sad. This would be

the real tragedy, would it not? To see another soul in pain and not be able to offer consolation? It is better to receive consolation from a soul who has experience with the trial you are enduring. You understand this, I know. So do not begrudge Jesus this time of sadness in your life. Through it He will bring the greatest benefit to your soul. I know that you might not agree with me but that is because you do not see what I see. I am in heaven and I see far more than you are capable of understanding. So perhaps you will trust me, and respect that I have the greater vision. If you walk through your dark period with Jesus, He will sow seeds of the greatest holiness in your soul. He will nourish your soul and tend to it lovingly. At the end of the trial, you will be a different person in that you will have a far greater capacity to house heaven in your soul and allow heaven to flow through you. You will benefit from this trial. This is truth. You will benefit. Will you benefit from an earthly perspective? No, my friend, not unless it is a Christian earthly perspective and then the benefits will be recognized. But generally, your world sees suffering as bad and to be avoided. We, on the other hand, see suffering as heavenly exercising or training, which conditions a soul to detach from the world. If Jesus needs you at a higher level of holiness, and He seeks to do this through suffering, can you really object? I hear that you are saying, 'Yes, Paul, but enough. I need relief.' Jesus knows what you can bear. Again I say that you should ask Him for relief. But do understand that there are benefits to your suffering that you cannot see. I love you and send my courage to you. I am asking Jesus to send you my joy also, because despite my great sufferings on earth, I had great joy. God's peace be with you always."

Blessed Mother

"My dearest little child, you need not be so sad. I am with you and I will take care of you. When you do not feel heaven's presence, it is only because you have turned away. It does not mean we are not there with you, interceding for you, watching you closely, and protecting you as you suffer. I love you most tenderly and I see that your heart is heavy and burdened. I do not like to see anyone suffering, ever, but I understand that it can be heaven's will. I watched my poor little Son suffer terribly, and while I objected through my entire soul, I understood that heaven's plan was more important and more productive than a mother's plan. God's plans must always come first, of course, if we are followers of God. And there is no other way to happiness. Please, dear child of heaven, trust me that I will remain with you through your cross and that I will obtain all that you need to persevere through this trial. I will help you in many quiet ways that you cannot see. I will always be there with you. Seek out my assistance. I will go to the throne of God and bring you with me. I will say, 'God, our good Father, please grant this treasured little soul everything needed for peace and calm.' God is so soft-hearted. He will not refuse us. I am your mother and I understand your pain. I am here to help you and you must believe that you are cherished by heaven. I trust my Son in everything. So must you. You cannot know the totality of His goodness or the totality of His love for you, but you will believe your mother when she tells you that you should place all of your hope in Him."

Heaven Speaks About Divorce

Jesus

August 5, 2005

"I speak today with such love in My heart. My love overflows. It is for this reason that I come to you to talk about the sad situation of holy marriages ending in divorce. I tell you why this grieves Me. There are many situations in which the marriage did not have to end. I am Jesus. I am God. I can heal many wounds if I am allowed to minister to the husband and wife in their difficulties. Every marriage will experience times when either one or the other is angry and would like to separate. This is to be expected and should not startle or frighten those involved. During these times, if the couple comes to Me and asks for My grace, I will send the grace necessary to preserve the family. Dear children of God, there are many reasons why I wish to keep families together. I am speaking to you today in general terms, understanding that there are times when a union cannot be preserved. I do not sanction violence of any kind by one party against another. This is not from heaven and heaven does not prompt either a husband or a wife to abuse. This comes from the enemy of marriage. In cases such as this, or in cases where one party has committed every effort to retain the

union but to no avail, My Church enters, with all of Her wisdom, and makes a decision. This is the way I have organized the resolution of these matters. My Church is given great wisdom and discernment and you should understand that by My Church I am referring to the priests who work for Me in the Church and who are obedient to their Pontiff. Bring your difficulties to Me, dear brothers and sisters, and I will help you."

St. Anne

"This mission, ordained by heaven, is a mission of mercy and healing. For this reason, I would like to encourage all who read these words to ask right now for God's mercy. Healing graces flow into the world in an amount that is unparalleled. So ask Jesus for these graces and He will send them. Dear brothers and sisters, there are many consequences of the disobedience that is prevalent in this age. One of the consequences of the darkness is the dissolution of so many marriages. When a marriage ends, there is great despair because most souls enter a marriage with the intention of doing good for each other and for any children sent. The bitterness that results from betrayal is profound. This bitterness is taking many souls down a path of self-destruction. The first thing you must understand is this. Jesus loves you whether you are in your marriage or out of your marriage. The love of your God does not change. Jesus does not reject a soul because the soul is divorced. On the contrary, Jesus sees that your hopes for your marriage have been disappointed and He rushes in to console you. You must come to Him all day long when you are suffering this terrible pain. Do not try to walk through this alone as you may then be drawn into behavior that will pull you further from Him and further from your heavenly dignity. Let the love of heaven wrap itself around you in your pain and you will recover. Seek the wisdom of a holy priest. Pray for the protection of your former husband or wife and be very alert to the needs of children who are part of the family that has splintered. These are not ideal situations, as you all know. We cannot pretend differently because that would be false. But it is especially in these situations that heaven flows in with abundant graces for all concerned. Remember that you can be sad and downhearted but still have peace. You are part of the heavenly family. You are a child of God. Peace is yours, my beloved soul. You need only ask for it in prayer."

"Children must have explanations in these cases. Do not think that the end of a marriage is the business of only the two adults involved. Where there are children, these little ones have a right to explanations, however simple and short. Many children feel that their parents are divorcing because of their flaws. Children often think of their acts of disobedience, normal in every child's life, and become convinced that these acts disrupted the peace in the home and caused a parent to leave. You, God's child, should understand that this causes the greatest distress in a child, even if that distress is hidden. You must believe me that this feeling is present in many children and you must give the child the information he or she is entitled to. A child should be told that heaven loves both the father and the mother and heaven loves all children, everywhere, regardless of their mistakes. Explain that the family should pray to heaven that all members find peace and happiness, together or separated. The children *should know that others suffer in this way also, and that heaven steps in very strongly to comfort and heal every person in this family that is struggling. In the end, through prayer, there will be peace and this family will be joyful together in heaven, with all bitterness healed. Souls are often doing the best they can in these difficult circumstances and there should be no blaming. I plead with you all today to spare your children any experience of hatred for their father or mother. This is unmanageable to a child. Children simply cannot cope with such things and their little souls become injured. Come to heaven in these cases and we will step in powerfully."*

"When a marriage ends, both the husband and the wife suffer. Both will carry a cross from this situation. It is good to remember when you are helping someone who suffers in this way that there are two wounded souls. One party may want the separation more than the other, it is true, but that does not mean that this person is not also in pain. It is very disappointing to heaven when people close to the couple join in and spread bitterness. This is a sad situation, yes, but that does not mean that a heavenly approach is not available. Do not judge. Children of heaven, I would like to repeat that sentence but I do not want to bore you. I will simply ask that you be careful to allow heaven to understand the situation. Content yourself that you do not. It is not necessary for you to judge. It is necessary only for you to love this couple and support their family. This is the heavenly way. When a husband loses a wife and a wife loses a husband, the grief should not be compounded by either soul losing their Christian family, who is called upon to support them in a profound way during this time. The wrong thing to do, which disappoints heaven, is for souls to consider themselves better

"Children of God, there is no ugliness that I have not heard. I see that souls are hesitant to bring certain problems to heaven's attention because they fear they will offend heaven. Well, how silly is this. Heaven is filled with souls who walked the earth, so heaven has seen and heard everything. You will not shock me, my beloved friends. If you are to heal from great pain, you must bring it to us. I am St. Anne and I want to help with these problems. Sit in silence and allow us into each sorrow, however ugly. Where is the correct place to bring such pain? If you do not bring it to us, you may bring it to a soul on earth who does not have the love or understanding to help you. You have experienced this, I know, and it is for this reason I talk about it. Family members often pile on additional hurt, simply because they do not know what to say to console you or how to deal with the issues. They can also find fault with you where none is indicated, which will be like piling great weights onto your already weighty cross. Seek your counsel most carefully during this time. Sit with Jesus, truly present in the Eucharist, and He Himself will listen to every pain and hurt. He will take it all and place it into the fires of His Sacred Heart, leaving you free to continue your beautiful walk up the mountain of holiness. It is like standing in a big mess. When you bring it to Jesus, He pulls you away from the mess and, with a glance, reduces the mess to nothingness. He is your healer. He is your trusted friend who will not make your cross heavier. He will make it lighter and manageable. Do you understand, my poor little hurt apostle? Seeking consolation in many conversations does not help. Trust us here in heaven and ask us to help and we will. Alert your guardian angel that you are vulnerable and need extra protection. This angel knows this anyway and grieves for your pain, but conversing with God's angels promotes heavenly thinking. All is well, children of God. Jesus fixes everything."

Blessed Mother

"My little doves are struggling. How earnestly I want to assure you that heaven has the graces you need. Dear little families, bring Jesus to your center and you will persevere. In most cases, marriages do not have to end. There is sufficient grace available to heal wounds and restore the sacramental unity. Often it is simply a case of one soul rejecting Christ, leading to all manner of pain and injury. Even in the most difficult cases though, heaven is prepared to step in and heal. I would like to say that many marriages are ill-advised in that one soul or the other is not following heaven and therefore not open to the graces that are necessary to preserve peace in the union. Well, dear children, how can heaven sustain a union when only one party is willing to allow direction? You see that this is a handicapped union from the beginning. So urge all to consider carefully before entering into the Sacrament of Marriage. In the cases where the marriage has ended, be docile to the Church and Her precepts. Do not talk rebelliously about the Church or blame the Church for the situation you are in. I, your heavenly mother, will help you to arrive at your destination, which is unity with Jesus and His Church. Seek the counsel of your priests and understand that Jesus is walking through every single moment with you. Be at peace. Know you are loved. Bring everything to heaven and you will not be disappointed. I will care for your family and protect your children and you will know the healing power of my Son. Your mother loves you and understands everything. Place your hand in mine now and we will walk courageously together through everything."

Heaven Speaks to Prisoners

Jesus

July 25, 2005

"I wish to talk to those imprisoned, for any reason. Dear brothers and sisters, your Christian family needs you. Your prayers, your sacrifices have great power. If you unite your suffering to Me, I can use it to save many souls. For example, if you offer Me each day, I will take your offering and I will use it to soften the hearts of your family members who are separated from you. I will use your offering to undo any damage that your sins may have caused. I do not need to say that I will work miracles in your soul. I do not need to say that because you know this. It is part of My promise to all lay apostles. You have not lived a perfect life, whether or not you are guilty of the crimes for which you have been accused. Even if those crimes were not at issue, you have not been perfect. How do I know that? I will tell you. No man or woman is perfect. All are sinners. In My eyes, this makes you no worse than someone who is not imprisoned. Do you understand? You may feel the eyes of the world upon you in condemnation, but in the eyes of heaven you do not stand out. You are My friend. I am your friend. There are many souls, not in prison, who are far guiltier than you. You are cherished and it is that

which I have come to tell you. Rest your head against Me, your Jesus, and I will heal you."

St. Francis of Assisi

"How can people be free, even while mankind has incarcerated them? I will tell you. The world can imprison your body, dear friends, but nobody has the power to lock up your soul. Your soul belongs to Jesus Christ. He, God, created you to serve heaven. Well, that has not changed simply because you find yourself in prison. It is all about heavenly service, so you must assume that Jesus needs you to serve exactly where you are. There may come a time when you are released from this prison and then you will be called to serve in another place. For now, you must serve where you find yourself. I want to tell you many things. The most important thing for you to know is that you are loved, just as you are, in whatever condition you are in. Jesus loves you. Jesus, who is all love, is also all mercy. He forgives you any sins you have committed. This is not conditional upon anything but your repentance. In other words, you may feel that the scope of your sin is great. You may feel that you have sinned so badly, and so often, that Jesus could not be talking to you when He offers forgiveness. Dear brother in Christ, may I say that this will not be the first time you have been wrong. I am telling you the truth. Jesus has forgiven you. Go to Him now and tell Him you are sorry. He is God. He has a right to your repentance. Understand that you must do this for Him. If you repent, and say you are sorry for your sins, Jesus will heal you of any marks on your soul left by these sins. Many times on earth a human being

experiences pain. There are many types of pain, of course, but the pain of not being loved or cared for is particularly troubling to a soul. This pain can then create a predisposition to commit sin. This may have been your situation. Jesus understands. Regardless, mistakes are mistakes and souls have to accept their mistakes, confess them if they are sins, and move on. Move on with Jesus. He holds His hand out to you in brotherhood and in love. Take His hand and step away from darkness, into the light. This is not a mistake. This is the wisest decision you will ever make."

"It is good to understand that heaven is very available to someone in prison. Would you like to know why? I will tell you. Souls in prison on earth have lost everything worldly, if only for a time. When you die, dear soul, you will lose everything from the world and you will go to God. There are no secrets in heaven. All will know all. So there is no hiding. You have done this already in that your sin has been exposed to the world. Others, not imprisoned, have sins, as we have said, but their sins have not been exposed in the same way. So you are in a position for great holiness. The trappings of the world have been taken away from you. You are often in a far better position to obtain holiness than someone who is living away from Christ in the world. You know of souls who love material things. They will have to learn to do without these possessions in heaven. You are practicing for heaven right now. If you were to die today, you would not have many attachments. I hope that you understand because Christ is calling you to a very close walk with Him. Also, Christ needs you and the family of Christ needs you. The world is suffering from the darkness of sin but Jesus is returning. He comes to bring heavenly light to this world and He is asking you to help Him do that. Will

you answer 'yes' to heaven? I, Francis, make this promise to you. Jesus will reward you more than you can ever imagine. He will give you far more in heaven than you lost on earth. This sadness you feel, this pain, will be forgotten. All of your pain will be gone. You will be joyful in heaven and you will be welcome in heaven. You will fit in with us, the saints, because you said 'yes' to Jesus today."

July 26, 2005

  "You may wonder how it is that you can serve Jesus while you are in prison. It is not difficult if you do it my way. In order to serve Jesus, you must become like Him. In order to become like Him, you must give yourself to Him. If you give yourself to Him, He will transform you into an apostle. An apostle behaves like Jesus, of course, or tries to, and I will tell you how Jesus behaves. Jesus never condemns a man who is repentant or even a man who desires to be repentant. So perhaps you are stuck at that first road sign. You see a sign that says REPENTANCE THIS WAY, *but you do not feel it. This is where the beauty of Jesus becomes clear. You can ask Jesus for even this. Tell Jesus that you want to be sorry but you do not feel sorry. Ask Jesus to give you sorrow for your sins. Ask Him to give you a spirit of repentance. Jesus will do this. He will do everything. Look up to Him and acknowledge Him as your King, your Savior, and your Creator. He will do the rest. Do you see that with Jesus, you cannot fail? You simply cannot fail.*

  "So you have repented for your sins. If you are a Catholic, you have confessed them to a priest, if possible. And now you are ready to proceed further on the path of the apostle. Here is the next step. You must rise each day, and give the day to Jesus. You do this through the Morning Offering. You offer

your day to Jesus Christ. And what does Jesus Christ do with this offering? He takes each action, each joy, each sorrow, each sadness and He uses these things to obtain graces for others who do not live in His light. Perhaps you were once in darkness. Someone offered his day, perhaps, and Jesus used the offering to obtain graces for you. And now you know Jesus and now you are living in His light. Do you see that we are all working for each other and we are all working for Christ? The most difficult thing for Jesus is to see even one soul lost for eternity. And during this time, many souls are being lost. This causes Him the greatest grief. You can help Him to pull souls back into the light by giving Him your day. You are suffering, are you not? If you are a soul living on earth, you are suffering in some way. So you can give Him your suffering. Unite it to His suffering on the cross. No man should be asked to die the way Jesus died. And yet, He did it willingly. My friend, He did this willingly because He loved you."

St. Thomas the Apostle

"How joyful I am that Jesus is allowing me to speak to you. I am with you, you know. We are all with you. There are many saints in heaven who spent time imprisoned on earth, for many reasons. You are called to be a saint. Do not even think that these words fell into the wrong hands and that they are intended for someone else. I am talking to you. Francis is talking to you. And Jesus is most certainly talking to you and trying to get your attention. So now that we have established that heaven is seeking you out, you have to make a decision. Will you decide for Christ or will you decide for

the world? There is only one God and He is Jesus Christ. He is the God in heaven, He is the God who walked the earth as a Man, and He is the Spirit speaking to your soul right now. It is that simple. You should not allow yourself to be confused. There is only one God. This God, this one true God, loves you. He knows everything there is to know about you and He loves you. He loves you so much that He has pierced the walls of your prison to bring you this message. The message is love. God is love. He loves you. You were created to serve and God needs you to serve now, today. You say, 'Maybe God does not exist. Maybe this man is wrong.' Well, to that I reply quite firmly. I am not wrong. I am in heaven. Heaven is real. And just as heaven is real, hell is also real. You do not want to go there, I assure you. So take your chances with me, Thomas, and I will help you get to heaven. Make your decision to serve Jesus Christ today."

"Do not expect to be certain about anything. You will have doubts. All great apostles served in constant doubt. When you die and Jesus comes for you, He will not look at your doubts. He will look at your service. He will look at your love. He will look at your pain and how you gave it to Him. If you are on earth, you experience loneliness. You will feel this way until you come to heaven. Every man feels lonely because they are not at home until they come to heaven. Some hide their loneliness through alcohol or other habits that numb this pain. This is the worst thing they can do because it pulls them further away from God and His kingdom. There is only despair at the end of that path. Perhaps you know this. Do not try to numb the pain. Feel the pain and then bring it to Jesus because He is the healer and He can eradicate your pain. The pain of separation from Jesus, when you allow yourself to feel it, is a holy pain. You want to

come to Him but you know that He needs you on earth, so you serve willingly, as He did. Be an apostle of service. There are others around you in pain, are there not? Perhaps you will bring Jesus to them. This is the same as taking a critically ill man to a doctor. It is an act of the greatest mercy. This is just one of the countless things you can do as an apostle of Jesus Christ. Come to me for courage and I will send you courage. Never fear man. Man cannot touch the soul. Only fear a permanent separation from Jesus."

"*If you want to know someone, you spend time with him. Well, we are telling you that you must become like Jesus. You will have to know Him to become like Him and you will have to spend time with Him to know Him. So each day must be spent in His company. He is with you and has always been with you. But you did not always recognize His presence. It is time to do that now. Talk to Jesus all day long in your heart. Ask Him what to do in each situation. Ask Him what to say in each conversation. Ask Him what He needs from you in every moment. This is praying. People tell you to pray all day. Souls think that this is impossible. But prayer is simply being with God. Talk to Jesus and He will explain everything to your soul. You will begin to change. Your bitterness will start to fade and you will feel your heart soften. This is not without some pain but this pain is coming because all does not remain hidden, as we have told you. You will have to face your hurts. Face them now with Jesus and He will take them away. He will leave you with a soul that is open to His love. Then, and this is the answer to all of the world's darkness, He will begin to flow through you into the world. Soul by soul, Jesus is returning. A great renewal is coming, my friend. Jesus is reclaiming this world for heaven. Will you help Him?"*

Blessed Mother

"I am with each of my children. As I am the mother
of Jesus, so I am also your heavenly mother. I do not
leave one of my own. How could I when I love you so
tenderly? Little soul, Jesus is so good. He is worthy of
your love and you will not be mistaken if you decide for
Him. I will help you. If there is something that you feel
is preventing you from coming to Jesus fully, bring it
to me and I will make certain it is taken away so that
you are not blocked from my Son. Cry out your sorrows
to me because a mother understands sorrow. A mother
is never too busy to listen to her child's pain and to
help that child move past his pain. Dear little soul, you
are cherished in heaven. Your soul is worth everything
to us. We will help you with each detail of your return
to Jesus. The saints in heaven watch carefully for an
opportunity to help you. I never leave your side. And
Jesus remains watchful, ready to rush in and fill you
with His light. Be very brave in your decision to serve
Jesus because the world would like you to reject Him.
But you will not. You will serve. We will send you all
you require. For now, you should rest in my motherly
heart. You feel my presence, do you not? That is because
I am with you, obtaining healing and mercy for you.
Peace, my little lamb, I am here."

Heaven Speaks to Soldiers

Jesus

August 11, 2005

"I direct these words today to soldiers, in every army, in every difficulty. Dear soldiers, I am with you. You find yourself in the most dreadful circumstances and often you fear for your soul. I am with you. I have the greatest graces available to you so that you can walk through your days with Me, Jesus. I see each decision you make and I understand that you are working under obedience to your superior. I am familiar with obedience. As you recall, it led Me to the cross. Sometimes on earth My children find themselves faced with situations that I never intended for a soul. All heavenly grace is with you, I assure you.

Here is what I am asking of you. Offer each day to Me. Pray for everyone you encounter in your day. Offer Me short prayers such as an act of sorrow if you are engaged in a battle where others are facing their deaths. Ask Me for forgiveness for every soul whose life is in danger. Ask Me to convert the hearts of those who are cold and those who are in a state of grave sin. Do you see that if you help Me with this, I can come into even the most horrid man-created situations with My healing grace? Dear soldier, if you are coming to Me, you have nothing to fear. Do not be afraid of death. If you are one of My friends, one of My apostles, and you must know that I consider you this way, you should have great joy and peace despite your surroundings. I have the most abundant graces available for soldiers everywhere. Many of these graces have been obtained by your family members who pray constantly for your safety. There are more angels and saints on a battlefield than you can imagine. Now be at peace and never think that I have left you because you are compelled to participate in a war."

St. Augustine

"My friends, we come to you in this way because you are being asked to behave in a manner that could be considered contrary to your faith. Blessed are the peacemakers. This is a true statement. And yet, you are confronted with war. Look through the past and you will see that history is dotted with wars. Jesus did not disappear or avert His gaze during these wars. On the contrary, how lovingly Jesus ministered to the souls caught up in these explosions of evil. There are many special graces for the souls who become immersed in such upheaval. You feel this to be true, I know. You see, there is great opportunity for holiness in these situations because you are forced to rely on Christ. When a man faces each morning without a reasonable expectation of living through the day, that man must contemplate God. The man looks away from the world, in his soul, and wonders what the next world will

hold for him. Jesus never passes up this opportunity. Your soul is transparent to us in that we wait for just such an opening. Heaven then rushes in and creates a wedge to keep your soul open. We, the saints, then obtain many blessings for you which can flow into the opening. Now there can be situations during war where the devil seeks to persuade the soul that God is not present and that the soul is condemned, given the actions that men are brought to during battle. This is not true. Jesus understands battle because Jesus understands everything. Jesus does not will war. This is contrary to heaven, always. However, there is a time when man must stand up against evil and that creates conflict. Again, heaven knows everything. You may wonder where you are in this war or that battle. I can only tell you that Jesus is with you. I could say it one hundred times, my friend, because this statement is such a blanket on everything we are trying to teach you. Jesus loves you. You are special to Him. He created you to serve heaven. He is sorry that you are in a situation that causes you distress. Jesus is with you. Jesus will never leave you."

"There is often a lack of justice on earth. Expect this. If you expect justice on earth you will be disappointed and embittered. A man of God, an apostle of Jesus Christ, should never become bitter. Jesus does not want this for you. If you are becoming bitter, you must spend more time with Jesus in your soul. You should never separate from Him, my friend, because bitterness and hardness of heart can come from great pain. Any man who has experienced war has viewed injustice. There is no justice in a child of God being slaughtered, whatever the reason. And yet, in war this happens daily. Should you become bitter because of this? No. If you are bitter, you are hurt. Bring the hurt to Jesus so that He can heal

it as you go. It will be more difficult if you leave it all to build up. Jesus makes all things right. So when you view injustice in your soldiering, ask Jesus to make it just in heaven. He will do so. This is what He does so He will hear your prayer and your request will add to the graces He lavishes upon those who are victims of injustice. Remember that most men are doing the best they can, given the circumstances in which they find themselves. Do not judge others. Why would you judge when you have Jesus alongside you to do that? It would be like thinking you can do a better job than God and I know you do not think like this. So let Jesus judge and do the best you can to bring Him into each situation. My dear friend, my fellow apostle, Jesus knows you do not want to hurt others. Jesus knows this. He knows you are often afraid and that you want to serve heaven. We are all with you in this. Heaven sees your anguish and feels the anguish of everyone around you, friend and enemy alike. Be more trusting than you have ever been in your life because Jesus will bring good, even from the bloodiest battle."

"A good follower of Christ always considers his death. And so we will consider your death, dear soldier. You are trained to live in a certain way. This is so that you will perform appropriately in situations where you are called to perform. So how does a follower of Jesus Christ prepare to die? Well, I must say that you should practice. Consider for a moment what will happen when you die. Your soul will leave your body and Jesus will be there. You will be brought into the light of Christ and the fellowship of those souls who have gone before you. Will you be afraid? Perhaps before you die, you will feel fear. This is normal. Accept this fear as your humanity rebelling against change. Pray at this time. Say 'Jesus, I am sorry for my sins. Please forgive me for any sins

*I have committed. Jesus, I trust in you.' Practice this, dear
soldier. Say it often during your days. You are walking with
Jesus, as we said, so do not be afraid to talk to Him. Tell Him
you are practicing for a peaceful death. He will applaud this
exercise and bring great graces of peace to you through it.
This is heavenly training and makes you a seasoned companion of Jesus. Do not fear death. It will be glorious for you.
It is a happy time for a friend of God. You will experience
this and you will say, 'St. Augustine was right. Truly he is my
friend.' Ask me for assistance, please, at any time. I will begin
immediately to secure graces for you. I want to help soldiers
learn about Jesus so that they can face their struggles with all
of heaven at their side. Your soul must be protected, especially when your body is at risk."*

*"Every human on the earth will die. This is a great truth.
It will not change. So you are no different than another man.
Every apostle of Jesus Christ is called upon to live the Gospel
message of love. You are no different than any other apostle.
So how can you live the Gospel? Offer Jesus your day and let
Him show you. You can bring His love and encouragement
to those around you. Many are in pain and spiritual darkness because they do not have His love. They have rejected
Him or they do not feel worthy to ask Jesus to walk with
them. Which man can say he is worthy? Certainly not I, the
man who speaks to you today. And yet, I am in heaven and
I am considered one of His friends. I assure you, He considers you in this way also, and your comrade who serves in
darkness is also one of heaven's treasures. Perhaps this man
needs you to bring Jesus to him. Perhaps he needs you to pull
him into the light. That is only one way you can live the
Gospel. Be patient in your struggles and inconveniences.
Offer them to Jesus. Jesus died for you so you must live for*

Him. You can do that in every little circumstance of your day. You can do it in hunger and cold, in fear and thirst. You can do it in loneliness especially because Jesus felt great loneliness on earth. All of these things make worthy offerings to your King. You will offer Jesus these things and ask Him to protect and convert your loved ones. He will do so. It is a mutual relationship in that you are offering something to Jesus and He is repaying you in magnificent ways that you can only begin to imagine and appreciate. Do you see that if we bring these words to others we will change the face of even war? Instead of an explosion of evil, we will have holy martyrs who have given Jesus everything, even their lives. I have told you that Jesus can bring good from everything. When I lived on the earth, I had only the barest understanding of that statement. From this, the heavenly view, I now see the extent to which Jesus will act to turn bad things to good. So be joyful, my friend. You walk in the company of heaven."

"I am going to begin a special prayer right now. I am asking Jesus to give you a small glimpse of the joy that awaits you in heaven. I am asking Jesus to grant this to you because I want you to be filled with hope and peace. When you experience the smallest taste of this joy, you walk differently through each moment. Sit quietly as Jesus places this in your heart. You know He is with you. You feel Him in your soul. Ask Him to come into your soul and remain with you. Jesus, in His mercy and love, will not refuse such an invitation. If you have worries about acts you have committed, tell Jesus you are sorry for having offended Him and then confess these things if you can. Receive His forgiveness and then walk away from these sins. Jesus does not want you to be saddened by the past. He wants you to be joyful about the future and peaceful in the present. There is nothing for you to fear.

Heaven awaits you. While you remain on earth, waiting for the heavenly summons, try to bring as many souls to Jesus as possible, even if only in the silence of your heart. This makes Him so happy, my friend. Each apostle has certain little ways he can serve in each day. These opportunities to serve heaven bring Jesus back into the world. If we have more apostles, the return of Jesus will come sooner and more powerfully. The suffering will be of shorter duration. Someone cared enough about you to give you this heavenly encouragement. Do the same for someone else. Bring us to earth each day, all day. All of heaven will rejoice as you seek our help. This shows God the Father that the souls on earth have not rejected Him. This shows our God that souls on earth love Him and seek Him and desire His help. God will reward you as He rewards each loyal apostle. The earth will become lighter and lighter as the darkness recedes. Now, I am with you and I love you. Ask me to obtain great courage for you and I will. Ask me for any kind of help you need. I will get it for you."

Blessed Mother

"My sons, my daughters, you are soldiers on the earth. I understand. But you are also my little children and I love you. A mother rejects any suffering for her children, and yet a mother knows that suffering will come to them. Remember that I am with you, as all of heaven is with you. Speak to us often and we will help you to make decisions. I can help to bring you to Jesus in your soul. This is what I do best because nobody knows the heart of a Son like a mother. Jesus is all good. He is all love. He is filled with forgiveness. You must never think that you cannot approach Him because you are sinful. All men are sinful, but Jesus forgives. Heaven would be empty if this were not true and yet heaven is filled with men and women, just like you, who are filled with happiness and peace. You will be here one day also, and I will be delighted to have you home safely. Now, you are heavenly soldiers also, so do not forget Jesus. You were placed on the earth, exactly where you are right now, to serve heaven, if only in your suffering. Place your hand in mine and I will bring you to God. I will say, 'Father, look upon this little apostle with great love, as I do.' How will God respond to us? What will He say? He will say, 'Mary, place this apostle here, in My heart, never to be separated from Me again.'"

Heaven Speaks About Stress

Jesus

August 9, 2005

"My children, why do you hurry so? Why do you feel you must move so quickly through your days? This is not the way I intended the children of God to live. You may tell Me that you have many things to do. I respond to you by saying that you are trying to do too much. You will not be holy if you move so quickly. I want My beloved apostles to move more slowly and thoughtfully through their days. I want you to make decisions on what I am asking you to do and what you are busying yourself with that is not from Me. I want your way of life to change and I am asking you to make this change now. In the next week, think about each activity and decide, with Me, if it is something I want you to do or something you want to do. My dearest apostles, I ask that you begin to remove activities that do not further My will. I want more time in silence, as you know. I want more time with families, without noise blocking you from each other. I want prayer, yes, but also conversations that are not hurried and stressed between husbands and wives, brothers and sisters, and parents and children. These are the souls I have decided you will walk through your life with and you have obligations to them.

If you are too busy with your own will, you are not seeing to Mine and you are missing opportunities both to learn from others and to assist others in learning about Me. If you do not pay heed to Me, who will? In order for the renewal to come, My beloved apostles must begin to seek only heaven's will in their days. And I am talking to you and calling you My apostle. Do not look to someone else or assume I am speaking to others. I am speaking to you."

St. Padre Pio

"Live simply. Eat simply. Love one another simply. Do not complicate matters unnecessarily. How do you live simply? You remove activities that are not necessary or that pull you away from duty. Consider your duty. Then move through each day and try to serve only that duty. Have order in your life and in the life of your family. There should be a rhythm to each day that does not change. Rise at the same time. Retire at the same time in the evening. Pray at the same time. This creates an environment in which you are free to consider God. Do not think, my friends, that you live in a world where the need for simplicity has disappeared. Apostles of Jesus Christ must set an example of service and obedience but not hectic service. There should be calm and if there is not calm in your life, change your life and keep changing it until you find calm. The act of sitting and reading these words is forcing you to consider heaven's wishes for you. Pull yourself away from the world even further and spend some

*time in silence when you are finished with reading. Ask Jesus
to show you which activities should be removed. My friends,
the lives of your children, if you are a parent, should also be
simple. Children should not be stressed by too many activities. They should have responsibilities in their home and
their parents should be present to see that the children meet
their responsibilities. This will make children feel good and
holy. If there is calm in the home, and not constant noise, a
parent is able to consider each child and see that each child
is proceeding in the acquisition of virtues. This is not happening if there is a constant stream of activity that prevents
souls from consideration of these matters. Live simply."*

*"Eat simply. There is a problem with eating and drinking
in today's world. There are those who are starving and those
who are gorging. My friends, I loved food when I lived on
earth. I loved it so much that I had to withdraw from it lest
I became too attached to it. Food is for sustenance. You
should eat simple foods, prepared at home, and not stress
your body with too much food or too much drink. This is not
how holy apostles live. Holy apostles consider what they need
to sustain their bodies so they can serve each other in physical strength. There is a time for feasting, of course, and these
feasts should be as generous as possible with great thanksgiv-
ing and joy. I am not saying that there should be no joy or
that food should be dreary. Mealtime should be happy and
cheerful. There should be prayers before meals and after
meals. These prayers should not be long or drawn out. They
should be simple and heartfelt, thanking heaven for provid-
ing for you on each day. What I am remarking upon is a distorted view of food and eating. If you are part of a family,
there should be others assisting in the preparation and serving of meals. Even if there is limited time, there should be*

some form of sitting together and ministering to one another with regard to each day's challenges or triumphs. If you are eating alone, this time of eating can be shared with heaven. It is heaven who is sustaining you, after all, so it is only just that heaven be given some attention. Eating should create a pause in your day. It is a time for reflection, a break between one task and the next, between one portion of your day and another. It is a time to consider your duty and how you are doing in the performance of it. Eating in haste is yet another example of how the enemy keeps God's children so distracted that they cannot consider Him or His will. Eat simply."

"Love simply. Serve each other in joy and patience. There is far too much talk about relationships. You were created to serve, dear apostles. Serve. Do not keep scorecards of who is serving the most or who is serving the best. You have only to account for yourself, so why do you concern yourself so often with the lack of service in others? Set an example of consistent service and you will find that others fall into line with you and improve. Love each other as Jesus loves you. Jesus forgives and forgets. Jesus does not wait to catch you at a bad moment when you are not doing your best or when you are discouraged. Jesus encourages you and overlooks your flaws. Do this for others, most particularly the souls who are called to walk through your life with you. No judging, my friends. Judging is for Jesus. Put the best possible light on others and expect the best from them and you will not be disappointed. Love passionately in that if you are called to walk with someone, be loyal to him as Jesus is loyal to you. Look for ways to make him feel cherished and appreciated. Small acts of kindness can change someone's life. Heaven is promising the greatest graces for this time. Heaven speaks the truth, always, and will deliver these graces. Ask for great

graces for each soul in your life, particularly that soul who is annoying to you or the soul you feel is failing you in some way. Ask heaven to surround him with grace and then love him. Dear parents, love your children simply. Look at each child as God's precious gift, created to serve the kingdom. How will that soul be called to serve? Each call is individual but I can tell you this. If there is a child in your life, you must consider what you are being asked to contribute to that child's formation. I am speaking now to all people, not just parents. Take an interest in the children around you and see what Our Lord is expecting you to provide in the way of encouragement. Brothers and sisters, serve each other in peace and do not fight and bicker so much. Love simply. Heaven will help you."

"Be at peace in the crosses God has asked you to carry. Do not be angry at heaven or blame heaven for the troubles in your life. Your life will end and the troubles will end. If you are at odds with heaven, your anger is misplaced. Brothers and sisters, neither should there be so much energy scrutinizing what your Church has done wrong. Acknowledge the mistakes of others and pray for them. Protect yourself from their flaws if they are dangerous to you, but do not live your life discussing the flaws and mistakes of those in the Church who are struggling. This is over. The time for this has passed. A renewed Church is coming, faithful and united, and you must help to usher this in by setting an example of great loyalty and fidelity. Perhaps there are things you do not agree with about this Church. Heaven accepts the fact that you have opinions. But you should discuss these things with Jesus and not use these points to pull your Church down and distance others from obedience. You will be accountable for this, my friends. If Jesus is calling you to lead in the Church,

then you must lead. If He is calling you to follow in the Church, I suggest you follow or risk displeasing heaven. These words I say to you are serious and I am praying that you will heed them. God is allowing this because He loves you and He does not want you confused and distracted. This relentless criticism of the Church is not from God, of course. But you know that and you understand that being in a constant state of disagreement with your Church is causing you unnecessary stress. There are many beautiful and brave souls who have been called to the renewal. You are one of them. Work for your Church and defend Her in whatever way you are called. This is God's one true Church and that has not changed. Be faithful during this time and your reward will fill you with the greatest joy. It is too uncomfortable for you to be doubtful of Our Lord's leaders. So you should be accepting of both your personal crosses and also accepting of the crosses your Church is carrying during this period. Heaven is with you in each personal cross and heaven is working to renew the Church. Be patient and calm while we work together in these matters."

"My brothers and sisters have many ways of dealing with stress in their lives. What heaven is trying to tell you is that much of your stress can be alleviated by a few simple decisions. The first is a decision for Jesus, total and complete. This will actually reduce all of the stress in your life because you will begin to live for heaven and not earth. You will concentrate on your duty, ordained by heaven, and not on the busyness that the world is trying to substitute for your duty. You will decide to live simply, eat simply, love simply and heaven will surround you with graces each day. Jesus will not be in one box and your life in another. Jesus and your life will be together each day, all day, and each decision will be made

in union with Him. This is service to heaven and unity with heaven. Concentrate not on how others are loving you or not loving you. Jesus loves you enough for everyone on the planet with you at any given time. Concentrate on how Jesus is able to flow His love through you to others. This is the renewal. This is the process of the Second Coming which has begun. Jesus returns to the earth through each one of His beloved apostles. If you are thinking that perhaps you are not called to be His apostle, let me clear that up immediately and state, with all certainty, that Jesus is calling you. You are called. You must answer. Follow Him and you will find your stress fading away, even in the greatest of trials and temptations. I am your friend and heaven is filled with souls like me who are also your friends. We will help you with the process of reducing stress in your life. Acquire a heavenly rhythm to your days and watch what Jesus can do. I love you."

Blessed Mother

"My little children become unhappy when they are too busy. They do not have time to give love to each other and to receive love from each other and this makes them troubled. They then seek to make themselves feel better by distractions that are not from God. Dear children, I am your heavenly mother and I will help you with this problem. Jesus wants you to live happily, even with the inevitable crosses that come in your lifetime. Be aware of each act that pulls you away from your duty. Be disciplined in organizing your life so that there is order and peace in your home. Do not allow possessions to clutter your home or your heart. Remove these material things and let your home be clean and orderly, as best you can. I am not asking that you be rigid, my dear children, but that you be simple. I am not asking that you be harsh with your children but that you set an example of order so that they will understand that too many possessions are not necessary. I will help you to be at peace with each other in your home. Please do not shout at each other. When this happens, and impatience takes over, apologize as quickly as possible and restore peace. Do not live in coldness. If there is a disagreement and you make peace, even if you are not at fault, all of heaven will applaud you. Blessed are the peacemakers, my children. This cannot be stated enough. Bring peace everywhere with you and you will be a faithful apostle of my beautiful Son, Jesus. I am with you and I will help you to understand how heaven is asking you to do this. Always look for the small opportunities. I love you. I will never leave you."

Heaven Speaks to Young Adults

Jesus

"I, Jesus Christ, cry out to all who read these words. Come back to Me. Come back to the side of goodness and kindness. I will send you every grace necessary for your complete healing and conversion. I will care for your every need. Trust Me, Jesus, and you will be saved. All is well. God's kingdom comes."

June 27, 2005

Jesus has revealed to Anne that He is beginning a lay apostolate for young people in the mission. This will be for souls after Confirmation until the age of twenty-four. Jesus will grant very special graces to these souls to assist them in rejecting the darkness.

"Through these young apostles I will flow powerful conversion graces to draw other young souls from darkness. My plan for young men and women is immense. Truly, the renewal will leap forward with the assistance of these individuals. Am I calling you? Yes. I am calling you. You feel the stirring in your soul as you read these words. I am with you. I will never leave you. Join My band of young apostles and I will give you joy and peace that you have never known. All courage, all strength will be yours. Together, we

will reclaim this world for the Father. I will bless your families and all of your relationships. I will lead you to your place in the kingdom. Only you can complete the tasks I have set out for you. Do not reject Me. I am your Jesus. I love you."

June 28, 2005

"My soul aches for the loneliness of this generation. Too many are unloved. Too many do not know the secure love of a holy family. Too many are unaware of the great love their God has for them. This must change. Dear soul of the kingdom, you are chosen to assist Me in this mission of love. You must bring My words to others. Do you know of someone who is sad and struggling? Do you see pain or bitterness in your friends? Bring My words to them and I promise you that I will minister to their souls. I will surround them with heavenly love and tenderness. Any mistakes they have made will be forgiven. I do not seek to condemn anyone. I came to the world to save souls, to rescue them. I am returning to the world to reclaim it for souls. You are My blessed apostle. You must assist Me. You know that I love you. I will heal you and place you on the path that is marked out for you. And then you must bring Me to others. You must comfort others with the comfort that was given to you. Will you do this for Me? I will do all of the work. You must allow My Spirit to reside in your soul and through this Spirit of truth others will return to Me. I am all powerful. I am capable of healing the most hardened sinner. You may think that you

cannot do this because the pain of others is too great. I assure you, little soul, even the greatest pain and bitterness is nothing for Me to heal. I have cleansed the darkest, most hardened sinners. And they became some of My most loyal servants. I am calling others from the darkness. And I am using you to do so."

June 28, 2005

"Great light is piercing the darkness of sin. I am that great light. I, Jesus Christ, return to the world through the souls of My faithful apostles. The first apostles were given all they needed to spread My Church. You will be given all that you need to reclaim My Church. In order to be effective as a young apostle, you must live your faith. The world would like you to believe that you can make any choices you are inclined to make. Dear apostles, this is not true. I, your God, have given you many choices. But it is never the right choice to sin against Me. It is always a mistake to commit sin. Do not be led by the world. Be led by Me. Be led by My Church. You say that My Church is not always good. There are those who have betrayed Me and damaged My Church. This is true. There will always be those who choose sin. Do not concern yourself with that because now is the time for us to renew this Church. And I need you to do that. I want you to be a carrier of My light, My truth. I want others to look at you and say, 'This Church must be a good thing. Look at the holiness of this apostle. Surely the joy in this

soul comes from God.' Do you understand Me, dearest? I am asking you to renew My Church. Where others have failed, you will serve. Where others have pulled My Church down, you will lift it up. Can this be a bad thing for you, to help Jesus? This can only be good for you, only right for you. You say, 'Yes, but Lord, what will I have to give up?' I assure you, you will give up only the things that hurt you and threaten to plunge you into bitter loneliness. The love that the world offers you is flawed. This distorted love leaves you sad. Live in union with Me. Live in unity with your Church. My graces will fill your soul and others will return to Me through you."

June 28, 2005

"My dear young apostles, how grateful I am to you. When many souls in the world seek only their own entertainment, you seek Me. This makes you different, of course. But My apostles in the world have always been different. What is the difference between an apostle and a follower of the world? I will tell you. An apostle is calm. An apostle is kind. An apostle spreads peace and justice. And an apostle leaves others with a longing for what is good. One who follows the call of the world spreads the opposite of these things. We will not name the fruits of the world because we want to spend as little time as possible with God's enemy. Dear young apostles, you must know the one you follow. How do you get to know a person? You spend time with that person. You converse

with that person. You think about that person even when you feel far away from him. And you begin to consider, in any given situation, how that person would view what you are viewing. Well, I would like you to know Me. It is really important that you know Me. My dear young apostle, you will spend eternity in My presence so you should be comfortable in My presence. If you are, then you will begin to absorb all of these heavenly gifts. Next, you will begin to love others as I love others. And soon you will look at this world and you will see what I see. Would you like to know what I see? I will tell you. I see a world hungry for goodness and kindness. I see a world that turns its face away from so much sin and darkness. I see a world full of souls who cast their eyes around in fear, looking for the One who comes to save. I am He. I am the One who has come to save. Walk with Me. You will learn how I wish you to serve."

June 28, 2005

"Have you ever seen someone in danger? Did you ever cry out sharply to prevent a friend from being injured? That is what I am asking of you today. I am asking that you look at your friends. If they are living a life suitable for a Christian, then all is well. You will share these words and you will share My joy. But if you see friends who are living away from Me and who are walking with My enemy, you must cry out sharply to them. Dear apostle, be very brave in this and under-

stand that all comes from Me. So you do not have to convince anyone of anything. You must simply do what I am asking of you. I am asking you to share these words with others. I will give you guidance. You will know who needs to receive My heavenly help through these words and graces. All of heaven is on your side, guiding you, directing you, assisting you in every way. We, your heavenly friends, will be certain that you know what heaven needs from you. Would you like a life without uncertainty? This is what I offer you. I offer you a life lived in the heavenly presence. You will walk with angels, dear apostle, because all of My apostles do so. You will have innumerable saints to call upon for counsel. All of My apostles have this. You will then have eternity to enjoy the fruits of your labors. This is what I offer to My followers. As the world becomes darker, your brightness will get brighter. You will serve with dignity. Truth will be yours and nobody in the world will be able to separate you from this truth. I am this Truth. Jesus Christ lives. Are you not proof of that? The hunger in your soul for goodness is proof of My existence. Look around for holy souls. You will see Me in them. I will be in you in the same way. My early apostles were not special in that they came from every different manner of living. I called them and they answered. I am calling you, and you will answer. Please help Me so that I can call out to others in the same way. I am relying on you, My beloved young apostles, to assist Me. I have great confidence in each of you. With Me, you cannot fail."

June 29, 2005

"You must draw close to Me, My dear apostles. If you are away from Me, you will begin to worry about what worldly souls think of you. And why does it matter? When you come to Me, as you will someday, do you think that I will ask you what others thought of you? I assure you, I will not. The opinion of others should not dictate your actions, except in the case of those I have placed in your life to give you guidance, such as your parents. If a soul is holy, that soul concerns himself with My opinion. He measures his actions against all that is heavenly and pure. He does not measure his actions against the world. Often the world will attempt to persuade you that sin is good, or at least an understandable decision. This is false. You know that. Sin is sin. Sin is wrong. Sin does you harm and can harm others as well. To commit sin against Me is to make the wrong choice. As a young apostle in the world, you will have many choices to make. You must make them with My counsel. I have the answers for your questions, My beloved one. I have all of your answers. You must come to Me in prayer so that I can give them to you. I am your first counselor. The path that I have marked out for you brings you to Me. And I am your goal, your destination. The worldly paths take you away from Me. They are the wrong paths. Many souls travel the worldly paths for years, thinking they will get back on the heavenly path before it is time to die. 'Well,' you might say, 'what is

wrong with that, as long as they get back in time?' I will tell you what is wrong with that. It hurts Me. This is rejection of Me and of My will. This, My beloved apostle, is why people are starving in your world. If you get on My path, the path that leads to Me, and the path that I have marked out for you, I assure you, I can feed the hungry and comfort all who are lonely. Do you see the plan? I intend to use you for these merciful acts. Say 'yes' to Me so that We can change this world."

June 29, 2005

"Do not be afraid. I say this so often to souls. There is nothing that should frighten you. I will protect you if you ask Me. If you are hurt or wounded, I will heal you. If you are struggling, I will assist you. If you are alone, I will comfort you and be your companion. Do not be afraid. Ask Me for courage if you are making a difficult choice and I will flood your soul with courage. With Me comes calm. With Me comes peace. I cherish you. Do you know that? I cherish you. I have created you exactly as you are. I take the greatest delight in your personality because through it I wish to flow into the world. You have been given gifts very carefully. You will need these gifts to serve Me in the way that I have decided you should serve. You have exactly what you need to help heaven. And that is why you are here in the world at this time. There are souls who have been destined to be helped by you. Will

you help them? Will you say 'yes' to your Jesus? If you do, you will have fulfilled your purpose here and earned an unimaginable reward. Dear young apostles of Jesus Christ, I tell you solemnly that often it will be the members of your own family you are called to assist. Are they in darkness? Are they in error? Do they need Me? You must bring Me to them. I will show you how. Perhaps it is simply through your example of peace and forgiveness. Perhaps you will share these words. Possibly you will serve them in more concrete ways, being helpful and cheerful. You bring Me to them by these actions and behaviors. If you help a parent, you are bringing Me to them. If you counsel a brother or sister wisely, you bring Me to them. If you alert your parents that a sibling is in trouble, you help Me. All of these things allow Me to flow into the world. Think small in terms of acts of kindness. Think big in terms of My power to change the world. Look into your life carefully, and decide what must change and how you can do better. I will be the one helping you to see clearly what is pulling you away from Me and what is drawing you closer. You are not alone. Do not be afraid."

June 29, 2005

"My dear young apostles, there are many things that I can teach you. If you spend time with Me, you will be loved, and you will then learn how to love. You will find that I am patient and kind. When you make a mistake, you will be forgiven

and we will move on. I will forget your mistakes. You will use the Sacrament of Confession to cleanse your soul and I will fill it then with beautiful graces, which will speed you on your path to holiness. I am a good friend, always. I listen and I love. I see your soul both in terms of where you have been and in terms of where you are going. Often you do not know where you are going. So My advice, given My knowledge of My goals for you, is crucial. You need Me, dear young apostle. You need My wisdom and knowledge. The more time you spend with Me, the more I can give you these things. You will become like Me. You will be a good friend to others. You will listen and you will love. Others will seek your counsel because they will come to trust you. What they will really be trusting is Me, because if you are united to Me, I can guide others through you. Do you begin to see the plan? I want to be close to you, indeed united to you, and then through you I will go out to others. Dear soul, it is only through unity with Me that you will have true peace. The world offers you darkness of spirit. Look closely at those who follow the world. Do they have peace? Are they loved? Do they sit calmly with others and allow others to speak, understanding that each soul is precious? You will find, I am sure, that those following the world are cynical. This suits them because if they are cynical they can justify their selfishness. Reject this. Reject cynicism. There are many Christians in your world and these followers of Mine are not cynical. They are warm and loving and kind. And this is what I want for you. So I love you and you love others. It is very simple."

June 29, 2005

"My dear young apostle, as a follower of Jesus Christ the Returning King, you are entitled to joy. I am returning to your world, and in this initial phase of My return I am returning through you. You should be joyful. If you are not joyful, you are spending too much time on worldly thinking. Think in terms of heaven and you will feel joy. Should a soul who is surrounded by angels be dismayed? Should a soul who walks in the constant presence of Jesus Christ be sad and fearful? My loving smile is in your soul. I hold only good wishes for you. There are many here in heaven who struggled with your very same struggles. They overcame the world and so will you. If you think it is too difficult then you are trying to do too much at once. Sit peacefully now, in this moment, and allow Me to calm you. I send My strength into your soul. I send you great trust in Me and in My presence. I am with you right now, watching you carefully, giving you exactly what you need to convert your heart to Mine. Stay in this moment and you will be fine. When you are anxious, you must see that you are either in yesterday or in tomorrow. I have given you what you need for now. Tomorrow you shall have what you need for tomorrow. Each moment is being seen to by heaven. I am not in yesterday, dear soul, because I am with you and you are in today. I am

not in tomorrow, dear soul, because I am with
you and you are not there yet. When you get there,
I assure you, I will be with you, regardless of how
difficult that day may be. I do not leave My
friends when troubles come. Rather I give more
graces. Many of the young people in the world are
feeling constant anxiety. This does not come from
Me. This does not come from following Me. Often
it is a lack of love and security. But, My dear
apostles, I am the only true security. Rely on Me
and you will find that your anxiety begins to
diminish. Soon it will disappear because I will
take it away. Ask Me for this. And then trust Me.
Many great saints spent their lives working on
trust. You will get better and better at trusting
Me through practice. And your fears will get
smaller and smaller. I can promise you this
because it has always been this way. Those who
live in unity with Me are at peace. The world cannot touch them because their sights are set on the
next world, their true home, which is heaven."

June 29, 2005

"Many of My young apostles are unfamiliar
with the saints who have gone before them.
These men and women have fought the same battles that you are fighting. They are here, in
heaven, with Me. But they are also with you in
that there is no separation of souls. When your
time on earth is finished, you will understand
more, of course, but for now what I want to convey is the help that you have. A saint in heaven

who has struggled with your struggles watches you closely, alert for a chance to assist you. He can obtain for you, through his prayers, a bit of clarity in a situation that is confusing you. He can obtain peace in a situation that has you disturbed. He can get guidance for you if you are facing a decision. Imagine it this way. You fight your battles and finish your work on earth. You come to heaven and join us here. But you still watch events on earth carefully. Now let's assume that you have served Me well, because you will, My friend, so I will be indebted to you. I will owe you for your loyalty. From heaven you see a young soul on earth who is fighting to overcome a problem. You say to yourself, 'Poor soul, I remember that struggle. I know exactly what would help that soul.' You come to Me and say, 'Jesus, please give me this grace for this soul who is struggling. I know what would help him because I myself struggled that way.' Because I owe you for your allegiance, and because you are My friend and I trust you, I grant your request. I give you this grace. Now maybe the soul you are watching is living in darkness, serving the world, and does not want My help or My love. Maybe that soul is even working against the kingdom of God. This soul is rejecting Me. But I look at you, My beloved apostle, and I cannot refuse you, so I grant the grace and the soul on earth is led toward the light. This, My dear young apostle, is how the Communion of Saints works. We were talking about a soul who is not serving the kingdom. Can you imagine how My saints assist a soul who is trying to serve? They stop at nothing to get graces for you. Ask them. Ask Me. If you do not know any saints, ask Me to send you one and I will reveal a saint to you who wants to help you. This may happen in many ways but I promise you that you shall have heavenly companionship and assistance. You are part of this family and this heavenly family works together."

June 29, 2005

"I want to speak to you about My mother, Mary. Mary is My mother but she is also your mother. She is your heavenly mother and will be your mother for all eternity. She is a powerful supporter of all of her children. The enemy scatters where this holy woman is welcomed because the enemy cannot remain in the presence of such purity. I am encouraging you to ask Mary, your Blessed Mother, for assistance in the area of purity. You are called upon to follow the rules of your Church in this regard. Sexual intimacy is intended for a man and woman who are in a holy union, in a blessed marriage. I am Jesus and I am telling you today that the rules have not changed. Do not listen to those who follow the world because you will be led astray. Listen to Me. There is grave damage done to souls because of sins of impurity. This sin leads to many other, even more grave sins. This is the sin responsible for the slaughter of so many unborn souls. Dear young apostles, work hard for Me in

this area. Do not let it be said that you sanctioned the murder of one of God's children. Speak out bravely here. If you have been led to this yourself, come to Me immediately. Ask My forgiveness. It is yours. I forgive you. I will make it right. I need to cleanse you of this so that you are not led to further sin because of your pain. Many, many souls have made this mistake and aborted children. This is the greatest indicator of the level of darkness in your world. But I have healing, even for this. Understand that I must have your help. I need you. You are not replaceable in this kingdom of God. Some of My closest friends working in the world today have committed this sin. Do I love them less? I am smiling, My beloved, because the truth is so far from that. Indeed, I do not love them less for their pain and their repentance. I love them more because they do not judge others. And they work for Me in the greatest of love. Work against sexual sin and work against abortion. This is always My will so you do not have to ask Me. It is possible that you will make mistakes in this area, even after you have committed yourself to be My apostle. I expect you to make mistakes at times and commit sin. Come to Me immediately and ask My forgiveness. Have your Confession heard as soon as possible after this. Together, you and I will minimize the damage of each mistake on your soul. We will together make the improvements in your soul which will help you avoid these sins in the future. Understand that I am with you everywhere. I do not leave when you commit sins because I must witness each act committed on earth. You have total love and understanding from heaven. You have total compassion. You have total forgiveness if you repent. And you will have complete healing for any past mistakes. I love you and you are Mine."

Blessed Mother

June 29, 2005

"My dear young apostles, how blessed is the kingdom of God by your presence in the world. You are a great joy to Jesus and you are a great joy to me, Mary. I want to help you. I want to protect you from harm. I can see difficulties for you even before you come upon them. Ask me for my assistance and you shall have it. Please pray the Rosary because the powers attached to this prayer will protect you. Through these Rosaries I bind you to my Immaculate Heart. In this way, I keep you close to me and I can steer you away from dangers. This prayer is being used by heaven to bind our apostles together all over the world. Through the Rosary, your hand is joined with the hand of each apostle on earth. Do you understand? The Rosary also creates an unbreakable bond with me, your heavenly mother. Through this bond I keep you and your loved ones attached to heaven. The world pulls at you but I am linked to you and so you cannot be pulled away. Pray the Rosary and I will keep you safe. I will help you to step over snares and walk around traps laid by the enemy. I will help you to heal. I will help you to see the world with the heavenly light that exposes sin, even when it is well concealed by those who wish to lead you away from me. I am your mother. I can only lead you to Jesus. This is my role. I bring souls from the world, see that they have what they require to heal, and then deliver them to my Son to serve Him. Use me to pull others from darkness. Use me to help you link up with souls also walking this path. Use me to steer you away from souls who will influence you against Christ and the path to Christ. This is my time in that Jesus relies on me heavily. I serve with the greatest of happiness because I love Jesus and I love you. Bringing you together is my joy. I work quietly, dear young apostles. I work in calm. I am gentle. You will not be wrong to trust me. Indeed, I am your mother and my love for you is complete. I hold you closely against my heart if you allow me. This is an exciting time and you are capable of tremendous good. I would like you to marvel at what Jesus can do with one soul. Look to your saints and you will see that with one soul, Jesus can topple a whole empire of evil. You are important. Heaven needs you. Come to your mother and I will help you to serve."

Part Five

History of
the Mission

From the Beginning

In the spring of 2003, at the direction of Our Lord, Anne began to record a spiritual journal. This would come to be known as Volume One, *Thoughts on Spirituality*. This was the beginning of her role as Anne, a lay apostle for Jesus Christ the Returning King

In July 2003 Our Lord indicated to Anne that her journal was to be published and disseminated:

July 23, 2003:

Jesus: "These words I bring to you are more good news. I want you to share these words, as you would share good news. If you prepare a great banquet, filled with the finest of foods, you do not sit down alone to sample and enjoy it. You invite friends and loved ones to share and celebrate together. In the same way, I want you to share My words. I will secure the necessary permissions and then you must obey the promptings I place in your heart. All will be seen to. I require only your obedience. I send these words to call humanity back to the light."

At this time Anne submitted the writings to Bishop Leo O'Reilly and her parish priest, Father John Murphy, and began to meet with both men regularly.

In August 2003, Anne's friend contacted Jim Gilboy, of Soul Assurance Prayer Plan, and asked him to consider publishing this journal. Jim indicated that he had no interest in publishing any other private revelations. He ended the conversation with "I work for Our Lady, so drop them off and I'll look them over." Jim reviewed the messages and met with Anne and after receiving permission from Bishop Leo O'Reilly, Jim printed Volumes One through Four.

Rome and the Personal Messages for Pope John Paul II

In January 2004, Anne recorded a series of twelve personal messages for Pope John Paul II. Per Our Lord's instructions, Anne asked Jim Gilboy to deliver them to the Holy Father. Jim agreed, although he had no viable connection to Rome at this time. Soon, though, a series of connections emerged and opened a path to Rome enabling Jim and a small group to meet at the Vatican with a Cardinal, a long-time friend of Pope John Paul II.

On Holy Saturday, April 10, 2004, the group met with the Cardinal and presented what is now Volumes One through Four of the series entitled *Direction for Our Times as given to Anne, a lay apostle.* Jim and the group explained that Anne received twelve personal messages for the Holy Father which they carried in a sealed envelope. The Cardinal asked many questions about Anne and her obedience to her bishop and the Church. The Cardinal was given the following message which Anne received before they left for Rome:

Jesus: April 5, 2004

"I would ask My servants to present these words as words from heaven. I have a great

mission that I wish to accomplish through these messages and I have attached graces that are unimaginable to human minds. Those who read them will understand if they have been called to participate in this heavenly project. Ask Me for guidance in this matter and guidance will be available to every person who pays attention to My will. Good and holy children of God, understand that these times are not like other times. These messages are not like other messages. I am trying to save many souls at this time. Do not think this can be done in the future. It must be done now. I ask that you treat this work according to My heavenly request for urgency. Your reward will be no small thing, even though I know you serve from love, not personal interest. Feel My graces flow through these words to your soul. Feel My truth as I convey it to you. All is well, as I am directing all, but I need many 'yes' answers at this time."

The Cardinal agreed to take the twelve personal messages to the Holy Father the next day at their brunch on Easter Sunday. The Cardinal kept a copy of the four Volumes as well as Anne's personal journal. The Cardinal directed Jim Gilboy to take a copy of the Volumes to then Cardinal Ratzinger's office, which he did.

On Easter Sunday, the group was privileged to sit on the same platform as the altar for Easter Sunday Mass. After Mass, they saw the Cardinal moving toward his van to attend brunch with the Holy Father. The sisters accompanying him carried the sealed envelope containing the personal messages for Pope John Paul II.

The following Wednesday, April 14, 2004, the group had a personal audience with the Holy Father following the general audience.

Publishing the Written Works

The Volumes

By the end of May 2004, publication of Volumes One through Four had been completed and the process of disseminating them to religious bookstores and the general public began.

In September 2004, Archbishop Philip Hannan of New Orleans, Louisiana began reading the Volumes. He was so inspired by these words from heaven that he decided his Focus Worldwide Television Network needed to play a role in getting the Volumes distributed quickly. He enlisted the assistance of Sr. Briege McKenna and Fr. Kevin Scallon to discern the content of the Volumes and make contact with Anne's bishop. After reading the Volumes and speaking with Anne's bishop, Sr. Briege was deeply touched. She encouraged Archbishop Hannan to proceed. Archbishop Hannan also spoke with Anne's bishop, met with Anne and filmed a series of interviews with Anne and her team. These programs launched the mission throughout the United States.

On October 15, 2004, Anne recorded the last message for Volume Ten. Jesus indicated that this body of work, The Volumes, was complete.

At the end of October 2004, two Sisters returned to Rome to deliver the remaining sets of Volumes to The Congregation for the Doctrine of the Faith and the Cardinal. The

Cardinal met with the Sisters and was given copies of the remaining Volumes Five through Ten. The following Sunday, October 31, 2004, the sisters were granted a private audience with The Holy Father, Pope John Paul II, in his papal apartment.

In October 2004, Volume Six was published.

In December 2004, Volumes Seven, Nine and Ten were published.

Currently Volumes Five and Eight are not in print. Anne's Bishop, the Most Reverend Leo O'Reilly, will decide when these Volumes should be printed.

In December 2004, due to the continued growth of the mission, Direction for Our Times emerged as a separate nonprofit organization. The organization was created to focus specifically on the mission of spreading the messages revealed to Anne, a lay apostle.

The United States office of Direction for Our Times is located in Justice, Illinois. The European office location is Bailieborough, Ireland.

Volume One:	*Thoughts on Spirituality*
Volume Two:	*Conversations with the Eucharistic Heart of Jesus*
Volume Three:	*God the Father Speaks to His Children*
	The Blessed Mother Speaks to Her Bishops and Priests
Volume Four:	*Jesus The King*
	Heaven Speaks to Priests
	Jesus Speaks to Sinners
Volume Six:	*Heaven Speaks to Families*
Volume Seven:	*Greetings from Heaven*
Volume Nine:	*Angels*
Volume Ten:	*Jesus Speaks to His Apostles*

The First Ten Heaven Speaks Booklets

In June 2005, Our Lord directed Anne to begin recording a series of ten short booklets for special groups of souls. These are called the Heaven Speaks booklets. The first ten are called:

Heaven Speaks about Abortion
Heaven Speaks about Addictions
Heaven Speaks to Victims of Clerical Abuse
Heaven Speaks to Consecrated Souls
Heaven Speaks about Depression
Heaven Speaks about Divorce
Heaven Speaks to Prisoners
Heaven Speaks to Soldiers
Heaven Speaks about Stress
Heaven Speaks to Young Adults

Direction for Our Times has published these booklets individually. Additionally, the messages contained in these booklets are printed in Part Four of this book beginning on page 135. These booklets are also available for free downloading, and printing from the website www.directionforour times.com. We encourage others to help us by printing and distributing them.

Climbing the Mountain

Nearing the end of the summer of 2005, Jesus brought Anne mystically with Him to heaven. Anne spent two weeks journeying and recording what she describes as "the tip of the tip" of what awaits us in heaven.

Following this, Jesus directed Anne to write about the lessons she has learned in her personal journey to sanctification. Here, Jesus gave Anne topics and asked her to write about them. This book, *Climbing the Mountain*, is the result of Anne's heavenly experiences and Our Lord's instructions.

The Newsletter

In September 2005, Direction for Our Times published the first quarterly newsletter. These publications contain articles written by Anne and other apostles, as well as updates on mission developments and events around the world. Each newsletter focuses on one of the Volumes and features the theme of one of the Heaven Speaks booklets.

The Mist of Mercy

As 2006 began, Jesus allowed Anne mystical experiences of purgatory. She then recorded these experiences. Next, Jesus asked Anne to write about spiritual warfare. These writings were published in the book *The Mist of Mercy* in July 2006.

Ten More Heaven Speaks Booklets

During Advent 2006, Jesus gave ten more Heaven Speaks booklets, telling Anne that this second group of ten booklets completed that series. Following are the subjects:

Heaven Speaks to Those Away From the Church
Heaven Speaks to Those Considering Suicide
Heaven Speaks to Those Who Are Dying
Heaven Speaks to Those Who Do Not Know Jesus
Heaven Speaks to Those Who Experience Tragedy
Heaven Speaks to Those Who Fear Purgatory
Heaven Speaks to Those Who Have Rejected God

Heaven Speaks to Those Who Struggle to Forgive
Heaven Speaks to Those Who Suffer from Financial Need
Heaven Speaks to Parents Who Worry About Their Children's Salvation

These booklets were published and made available in February 2007. They are also available for free downloading and printing from the website www.directionforourtimes.com.

In Defense of Obedience and Reflections on the Priesthood

This work by Anne, published in August 2007, consists of two essays on topics close to the heart of Jesus. The first is entitled *In Defense of Obedience* and the second is entitled *Reflections on the Priesthood.*

In Defense of Obedience is a serious call to return to a spirit of obedience to the Magisterium of the Church. Obedience to the Church is a must for every apostle, laity and clergy alike.

Anne's essay on the priesthood gives us the smallest glimpse of the love Our Lord has for the men who hear and answer His call. We read the depth of the connection Jesus has with these men and how they are united in a most unique way to the Sacred Heart of Jesus and the Immaculate Heart of Mary. This is also a gentle reminder that we are called to love and support our priests who serve us in their humanity but with a heavenly dignity bestowed upon them from heaven by Jesus Christ, the First Priest.

This is the complete list of published writings as of this date of publication in September 2007.

Monthly Message for the World

On December 1, 2004, Jesus began giving a monthly message for the world. He indicated that Anne would receive a monthly message from Him on the first of each month. These monthly messages are published on the Direction for Our Times website **www.directionforourtimes.com** and can be mailed in paper or electronic form to anyone interested.

Obedience to the Roman Catholic Church

Anne has submitted all writings to her two spiritual directors and her bishop, the Most Reverend Leo O'Reilly. She has also submitted all writings to the Congregation for the Doctrine of the Faith in the Vatican. Bishop O'Reilly has read each of these writings and has given permission that they be published and circulated throughout the world.

The Church examines reports of private revelation very carefully. To date, the writings and experiences of Anne, a lay apostle, indicate overwhelming evidence of authenticity. Included in this updated edition of *Climbing the Mountain* is a theological commentary written by Dr. Mark I. Miravalle, S.T.D. Professor of Theology and Mariology from Franciscan University at Steubenville (see page 271).

Jesus has revealed these works to assist us in our journey to unity with Him and in our labors for Him. One of the tools He is giving us, to assist us in the work He has willed for us in the renewal, is the messages recorded in these Volumes, books and booklets.

When you review the list and see the scope of the works, you will understand the determination evidenced by Our Lord to assist us at this time.

He is calling each and every one of us to work in this renewal.

The Formation of the Lay Apostolate of Jesus Christ the Returning King

In May 2005, Our Lord revealed to Anne a set of guidelines for those called to assist in the work of this mission. Bishop Leo O'Reilly gave permission for the formation of the Lay Apostolate of Jesus Christ the Returning King.

Anne received the following guidelines from Our Lord:

We seek to be united to Jesus in our daily work, and through our vocations, in order to obtain graces for the conversion of sinners. Through our cooperation with the Holy Spirit, we will allow Jesus to flow through us to the world, bringing His light. We do this in union with Mary, our Blessed Mother, with the communion of saints, with all of God's holy angels, and with our fellow lay apostles in the world.

Guidelines for Lay Apostles

As lay apostles of Jesus Christ the Returning King, we agree to perform our basic obligations as practicing Catholics. Additionally, we will adopt the following spiritual practices, as best we can:

1. **Allegiance Prayer** and **Morning Offering**, plus a brief prayer for the Holy Father
2. **Eucharistic Adoration**, one hour per week
3. **Prayer Group Participation**, monthly, at which we pray the Luminous Mysteries of the Holy Rosary and read the monthly message
4. **Monthly Confession**
5. Further, we will follow the example of Jesus Christ as set out in the Holy Scripture, treating all others with His patience and kindness.

Allegiance Prayer

Dear God in Heaven, I pledge my allegiance to You. I give You my life, my work and my heart. In turn, give me the grace of obeying Your every direction to the fullest possible extent. Amen.

Morning Offering

O Jesus, through the Immaculate Heart of Mary, I offer You the prayers, works, joys and sufferings of this day, for all the intentions of Your Sacred Heart, in union with the Holy Sacrifice of the Mass throughout the world, in reparation for my sins, and for the intentions of the Holy Father. Amen.

Prayer for the Holy Father

Blessed Mother of Jesus, protect Our Holy Father Benedict XVI, and bless all of his intentions.

Five Luminous Mysteries
1. The Baptism of Jesus
2. The Wedding at Cana
3. The Proclamation of God's Kingdom
4. The Transfiguration
5. The Institution of the Eucharist

Promise from Jesus to His Lay Apostles

May 12, 2005

Your message to souls remains constant. Welcome each soul to the rescue mission. You may assure each lay apostle that just as they concern themselves with My interests, I will concern Myself with theirs. They will be placed in My Sacred Heart and I will defend and protect them. I will also pursue complete conversion of each of their loved ones. So you see, the souls who serve in this rescue mission as My beloved lay apostles will know peace. The world cannot make this promise as only heaven can bestow peace on a soul. This is truly heaven's mission and I call every one of heaven's children to assist Me. You will be well rewarded, My dear ones.

Anne says, "Our mission as lay apostles is to climb the mountain of holiness concentrating on moving always deeper into the divine will and always further from self-will." It is hoped that every soul reading these words will begin to walk this path, taking full advantage of the graces heaven so generously lavishes upon us.

The Image of Jesus Christ
the Returning King

In September 2005, Anne received a series of locutions from St. Faustina:
"Anne, our missions are destined to be joined. Your mission is an extension of my mission in that it is all part of the Divine Mercy. Jesus has put a great amount of graces in the pot that is the Volumes. Regardless of how many souls dip their cups into this pot, they will come up filled with graces because the Lord has willed that the amount be limitless. . . . You have my personal commitment to assist you in this project and in every project. It is good you have come to know me, Anne, because you know that I understand your struggles. You can trust my advice in every situation."

The next month, October 2005, Anne was invited by Sr. Briege McKenna and Fr. Kevin Scallon on a brief pilgrimage to the International Divine Mercy Shrine in Krakow, Poland.

While there, Sr. Briege, Fr. Kevin and Anne met with the Mother Superior of the order to which St. Faustina belonged, The Congregation of the Sisters of Our Lady of Mercy. Earlier that morning, St. Faustina told Anne, *"Today I am going to link our missions."*

Sister Briege recounts what transpired:

"We explained to the sister who Anne was and spoke about the messages and her writings. Anne then began to tell the sisters about her experience with the Lord and most recently with St. Faustina herself. When she mentioned that her mission was to spread the message of Jesus Christ the Returning King, the Mother Superior told her about something very strange that had happened to her the day before. She explained that on her feast day an artist friend of hers had presented her with a painting, which he had told Mother Superior would be a painting of her patron saint. However, when he gave her the painting, he explained it was a painting of Christ the King. She immediately went off to fetch the painting and when we saw it, all of us in the room were amazed and recognized that this painting was to be the authentic image for the apostolate representing Jesus Christ the Returning King. The Mother Superior immediately presented the painting to Anne telling her she was certain that it was really meant for Anne. We all felt we were present at a moment of great significance which we will look back on with gratitude."

St. Faustina confirmed the importance of this image in a locution to Anne on October 28, 2005:

"The image of Jesus Christ the Returning King should be spread throughout the world. There are many graces attached to this image. Like the Divine Mercy image, this image will be widely recognized as a source of goodness and healing. All who venerate this image will be blessed. I am grateful that God allows me the privilege of assisting in this mission. Each apostle should feel the same way and each apostle should thank God for being chosen to serve. Such joy flows from heaven. Bask in the joy, dear apostles, because your King is returning."

Painting of *Jesus Christ the Returning King* by Janusz Antosz.

Saint Faustina Kowalska Speaks to Anne, a lay apostle

September 28, 2005

"The mercy of God cannot be measured in that the greater the pleas, the greater the mercy. So the amount of mercy flowing down into the world is directly proportional to the amount of pleas for mercy that come from the world. Do not think that Jesus will limit His mercy. His mercy has no limits. I am asking that each apostle plead with heaven for mercy. The Chaplet of Divine Mercy is an effective way to ask God for mercy and I encourage all lay apostles to use this heavenly tool. Indeed, it is for these times that the Chaplet was revealed. As you ask God for mercy, mercy will flow down into your world and each soul you encounter in your day will be the recipient of His mercy."

October 3, 2005

"Dear apostles, rest often in the limitless pool of God's mercy. Call this mercy down upon all sinners, all souls in error, all suffering souls and all apostles. The mercy of God floods the world in this time because God is good. When even one soul asks for mercy a floodgate is opened. Imagine, my dear apostles, if each apostle begged God for mercy. The world would change and I say this with the authority of heaven. There would be a detectable increase in peace and purity. It is for this reason that I am speaking to you today. I want the humble little Chaplet to be a weapon for each lay apostle. This will add great momentum to this movement because of the power attached to the Chaplet and because of

the great need for mercy in the world today. I will help each apostle in each heavenly project. I am a special friend to this mission and my loyalty is complete. Call on me for guidance and I will obtain it for you."

Monday October 24, 2005

"Dear souls, we must spread God's mercy throughout the world. All souls will have the opportunity to benefit from God's great mercy. Indeed, this opportunity is available in each moment of each life. God is patient and waits for the soul to turn to Him in need, in sorrow, in humility. When this occurs, God can flood the soul with His merciful healing. For this reason, you must assist in this mission. Ask Jesus what He would like you to do for the good of souls and He will tell you. All souls are necessary so you must understand that you have a role to play. I played my role in God's merciful plan while I served on earth. Now you must serve. Heaven is joined with earth and sends all necessary grace. When you are serving Christ, you will know peace, even in suffering. Do not be surprised when you carry a cross for Jesus. This is a sign that He looks upon you as a friend. Dear friends of heaven, this is a time for the greatest trust. So trust Jesus in your doubts and fears and sufferings and you will be making the right choice."

Eucharistic Days Of Renewal

As increasing numbers of people are drawn to Our Lord through these writings and called to assist in this rescue mission, leaders in Catholic communities began to ask if Anne could come and speak. With the permission of Bishop O'Reilly and the permission of the bishops in each hosting diocese, Anne began to lead Eucharistic Days of Renewal in the United States.

Her first Eucharistic Day of Renewal was in April of 2005 in Tinley Park, Illinois. As of February 2007, Anne has led Eucharistic events in many United States cities.

International Eucharistic Days of Renewal

At the request of Sr. Briege McKenna and Fr. Kevin Scallon, Anne has spoken each week at the Intercession for Priests held in Dublin for the last three years.

Anne traveled to the Philippines with her spiritual director, Father Darragh Connolly, for two weeks in November 2006, leading Eucharistic days of Renewal for priests and laity.

These days of Eucharistic Renewal included Mass, a Holy Hour of Eucharistic Adoration and a talk by Anne. Jesus promised a great outpouring of His grace at these gatherings and He has not disappointed.

More recently, as Anne has stopped traveling, Eucharistic Days are being planned in many places with other guest speakers. Additionally, many apostles are being prompted by Jesus to visit prayer groups and communities in order to share the good news given in the Volumes and writings of this mission. This is truly a heavenly call for modern evangelization.

Anne continues to receive requests from many countries to lead Eucharistic Days of Renewal. Anne is currently leading Eucharistic Days of Renewal in her diocese in Ireland.

An Introduction to Anne, a lay apostle

In 2003 Anne, a lifelong Catholic, began receiving messages that she eventually recognized as interior locutions from Jesus, Mary and some of the saints. A more detailed account of her life is found in the Introduction that is located at the front of each of the Volumes. A copy of this Introduction follows on page 253.

Under the direction of the Blessed Virgin Mary, Anne serves anonymously, as much as is possible. On April 16, 2005, Our Lady told Anne:

"I want you to retain your private life as a mother and wife. In order for this to be possible, souls must obey my instructions. Anne, you will speak for Jesus and represent this mission. When you are speaking, you are Anne. When you are working for this mission, you are Anne. When you are serving your family at home or away from home, you are a mother and wife and you belong to your family. Souls must be respectful of this because your vocation must be protected. If the situation arose that you were serving this mission and your family was suffering, we would take you from the mission. You have a heavenly duty, Anne, so please advise souls to be respectful. You will bring great graces to others but only through obedience to heaven. I will help you with each situation but we are serious about this distinction of service. Your family will not suffer. I am personally appealing to each soul to respect this woman's anonymity."

Anne has said the following about her role in this mission: "When you approach a castle you pay homage to the king, not the janitor. Don't write about me. Write about the lay apostles and the mission Jesus has for them."

Anne recently said this about the messages revealed in this work:

"Consider that Jesus Christ wants to talk to you. Allow for the possibility that He is doing so through these works. The consistent experience of people who have read the Volumes is, "I felt like He was talking to me." Well, He was. If you are interested to know what Jesus Christ has to say to you, pick up one of these works and see if the graces are there. They are so heavily weighted with graces. The words are recorded by a flawed human being, but the graces that flow through the words are heavenly and magnificent.

"There is a temptation for some people to focus on me because I typed the words for Jesus. This is a mistake. I am like every other apostle who is trying to serve Jesus in this time. I serve from within the ranks of the apostolate and pray that others will trust the priests chosen by the Lord to oversee and protect this mission, and allow me to serve quietly."

Introduction as Found in
Each of the Volumes

Dear Reader,

I am a wife, mother of six, and a Secular Franciscan.

At the age of twenty, I was divorced for serious reasons and with pastoral support in this decision. In my mid-twenties I was a single parent, working and bringing up a daughter. As a daily Mass communicant, I saw my faith as sustaining and had begun a journey toward unity with Jesus, through the Secular Franciscan Order or Third Order.

My sister travelled to Medjugorje and came home on fire with the Holy Spirit. After hearing of her beautiful pilgrimage, I experienced an even more profound conversion. During the following year I experienced various levels of deepened prayer, including a dream of the Blessed Mother, where she asked me if I would work for Christ. During the dream she showed me that this special spiritual work would mean I would be separated from others in the world. She actually showed me my extended family and how I would be separated from them. I told her that I did not care. I would do anything asked of me.

Shortly after, I became sick with endometriosis. I have been sick ever since, with one thing or another. My sicknesses are always the types that mystify doctors in the beginning. This is part of the cross and I mention it because so many suffer in this way. I was told by my doctor that I would never conceive children. As a single parent, this did not concern me as I assumed it was God's will. Soon after, I met a wonderful man. My first marriage had been annulled and we married and conceived five children.

Spiritually speaking, I had many experiences that included what I now know to be interior locutions. These moments were beautiful and the words still stand out firmly in my heart, but I did not get excited because I was busy offering up illnesses and exhaustion. I took it as a matter of course that Jesus had to work hard to sustain me as He had given me a lot to handle. In looking back, I see that He was preparing me to do His work. My preparation period was long, difficult and not very exciting. From the outside, I think people thought, Man, that woman has bad luck. From the inside, I saw that while my sufferings were painful and long lasting, my little family was growing in love, in size and in wisdom, in the sense that my husband and I certainly understood what was important and what was not important. Our continued crosses did that for us.

Various circumstances compelled my husband and me to move with our children far from my loved ones. I offered this up and must say it is the most difficult thing I have had to contend with. Living in exile brings many beautiful opportunities to align with Christ's will; however, you have to continually remind yourself that you are doing that. Otherwise you just feel sad. After several years in exile, I finally got the inspiration to go to Medjugorje. It was actually a gift from my husband for my fortieth birthday. I had tried to go once before, but circumstances prevented the trip and I understood it was not God's will. Finally, though, it was time and my eldest daughter and I found ourselves in front of St.

James Church. It was her second trip to Medjugorje.

I did not expect or consider that I would experience anything out of the ordinary. My daughter, who loved it on her first trip, made many jokes about people looking for miracles. She affectionately calls Medjugorje a carnival for religious people. She also says it is the happiest place on earth. This young woman initially went there as a rebellious fourteen year old, who took the opportunity to travel abroad with her aunt. She returned calm and respectful, prompting my husband to say we would send all our teenagers on pilgrimage.

At any rate, we had a beautiful five days. I experienced a spiritual healing on the mountain. My daughter rested and prayed. A quiet but significant thing happened to me. During my Communions, I spoke with Jesus conversationally. I thought this was beautiful, but it had happened before on occasion so I was not stunned or overcome. I remember telling others that Communions in Medjugorje were powerful. I came home, deeply grateful to Our Lady for bringing us there.

The conversations continued all that winter. At some time in the six months that followed our trip, the conversations leaked into my life and came at odd times throughout the day. Jesus began to direct me with decision and I found it more and more difficult to refuse when He asked me to do this or that. I told no one.

During this time, I also began to experience direction from the Blessed Mother. Their voices are not hard to distinguish. I do not hear them in an auditory way, but in my soul or mind. By this time I knew that something remarkable was occurring and Jesus was telling me that He had special work for me, over and above my primary vocation as wife and mother. He told me to write the messages down and that He would arrange to have them published and disseminated. Looking back, it took Him a long time to get me comfortable enough where I was willing to trust Him. I trust His voice now and will continue to do my best to serve Him, given my constant struggle with weaknesses, faults, and the pull of the world.

Please pray for me as I continue to try to serve Jesus. Please answer "yes" to Him because He so badly needs us and He is so kind. He will take you right into His heart if you let Him. I am praying for you and am so grateful to God that He has given you these words. Anyone who knows Him must fall in love with Him, such is His goodness. If you have been struggling, this is your answer. He is coming to you in a special way through these words and the graces that flow through them.

Please do not fall into the trap of thinking that He cannot possibly mean for you to reach high levels of holiness. As I say somewhere in my writings, the greatest sign of the times is Jesus having to make do with the likes of me as His secretary. I consider myself the B-team, dear friends. Join me and together we will do our little bit for Him.

Message received from Jesus immediately following my writing of the above biographical information:

You see, My child, that you and I have been together for a long time. I was working quietly in your life for years before you began this work. Anne, how I love you. You can look back through your life and see so many "yes" answers to Me. Does that not please you and make you glad? You began to say "yes" to Me long before you experienced extraordinary graces. If you had not, My dearest, I could never have given you the graces or assigned this mission to you. Do you see how important it was that you got up every day, in your ordinary life, and said "yes" to your God, despite difficulty, temptation, and hardship? You could not see the big plan as I saw it. You had to rely on your faith. Anne, I tell you today, it is still that way. You cannot see My plan, which is bigger than your human mind can accept. Please continue to rely on your faith as it brings Me such glory. Look at how much I have been able to do with you, simply because you made a quiet and humble decision for Me. Make another quiet and humble decision on this day and every day, saying, "I will serve God." Last night you served Me by bringing comfort to a soul in pain. You decided against yourself and for Me, through your service to him. There was gladness in heaven, Anne. You are Mine. I am yours. Stay with Me, My child. Stay with Me.

Part Six

Articles Relating
to the Mission

St. Faustina, Pope John Paul II and Anne, a Lay Apostle:

Three Servants of the Returning King

By Howard Q. Dee

This is a story of amazing grace, of three persons whose lifetimes overlap one another, spanning a period of over a century, working for the same goal under the direction of the same Master. The first is a cloistered nun who became a saint; the second a great Pontiff of the Roman Catholic Church; and the third a present day housewife and mother. Their common Master is Jesus Christ; their common goal: to prepare for His return to establish His Kingdom of justice, love and peace.

For almost twenty centuries, Christians have been awaiting the return of the Savior King. Even His own apostles thought they would live to see His return as He had promised.

While we pray for His return as an article of faith, "Christ has died. Christ is risen. Christ will come again," we no longer truly anticipate Jesus' return in our hearts, but consider it an event both remote and uncertain in time.

Father Raneiro Cantalamessa, preacher to the Pontifical Household, in his homily on the Feast of Christ the King, said: "A general atmosphere of impunity is established in today's society, in which there are competitions to break the law, to corrupt and allow ourselves to be corrupted, with the justification that 'everyone does it.' Is not this, in a certain sense, the situation in which we all live? One after the other, the commandments of God are calmly broken, including the ones that say, 'Thou shall not kill,' 'Thou shall not steal,' 'Thou shall not commit adultery,' with the pretext that 'everyone does it,' that culture, progress and even human law now allow it. But God has never thought of abolishing the commandments or the Gospel, and this general feeling of security is no more than a fatal deception."

"Some years ago, Michelangelo's fresco of the Universal Judgment was restored. But there is another universal judgment that must be restored. It is not painted on brick walls, but on the hearts of Christians. It has become totally discolored and is being turned into ruins. The beyond and, with it, the judgment has become a joke, something so uncertain that one is amused to think that there was a time in which this idea transformed the whole of human existence. There are those who might wish to console themselves, saying that, after all, the day of judgment is very far off, perhaps millions of years away. But from the Gospel, Jesus responds: *"Fool! This night your soul is required of you."* (*Luke* 12:20) Now is the time for mercy; then it will be a time of justice. It is for us to choose, while we still have time."

With that backdrop from Father Cantalamessa, let us proceed with our story.

The first Servant of the Returning King was a cloistered nun of the Sisters of Our Lady of Mercy in the city of Warsaw, Poland by the name of Sr. Faustina Kowalska. In the 1930s, Our Lord Jesus appeared to her and in a series of messages covering many years, asked her to promote the devotion to His Divine Mercy, in preparation for His return to earth. Heaven will open its gates for His mercy to flow during this allotted time which will then give way to a day of justice when He will come in glory. In 1938, Jesus told Sr. Faustina: *"I have a special love for Poland, and if she will be obedient to My will, I will exalt her in might and holiness. From her will come forth the spark that will prepare the world for My final coming."* Sr. Faustina died that same year and was buried on October 7, a First Friday, the Feast of the Holy Rosary.

Under Jesus' personal direction, the devotion to the Divine Mercy and the praying of the Chaplet of Divine Mercy would eventually spread to the entire Catholic world.

Now enters the second Servant of the Returning King. In May, 1938, a young Polish man of eighteen by the name of Karol Wojtyla, accompanied by his father, moved from their hometown Wadowize in Poland to the city of Cracow to enroll in the Faculty of Philosophy in Jagiellonian University. In 1942, during the Second World War, he entered the clandestine Cracow seminary, still unaware that he would be the "spark" that Jesus had chosen to continue this mission begun by Sr. Faustina to prepare the world for His coming.

Twenty five years later, in 1967, His Eminence Karol Cardinal Wojtyla, now Archbishop of Cracow, in a solemn ceremony closes the Informative Process of Sr. Faustina, Servant of God, as the first step towards her Sainthood. And 33 years later, during the Jubilee Year 2000, the same Prelate, now Pope John Paul II, Pontiff of the Universal Church, canonized St. Faustina, recognizing her forerunner role in preparing for the Second Advent.

When Pope John Paul II announced the Advent of the Third Millennium, he said that this was the hermeneutical key, the defining point, of his Pontificate. He called it the New Advent, the old Advent having taken place 2000 years earlier when the Savior King came as the Son of Mary.

In announcing the New Advent, Pope John Paul II said: "The Great Jubilee cannot be a mere remembrance of a past event. . . . It is to be the celebration of a Living Presence and to look towards the Second Coming of Our Savior when He will establish once and for all His Kingdom of justice, love and peace."

He repeated this theme of Jesus' return on many other occasions:

"We are not simply to believe, but to watch; not simply to love, but to watch; not simply to obey, but to watch; thus it happens that watching is a suitable test of a Christian. This is because to watch is to be detached from what is present, and to live in what is unseen, to live in the thought of Christ as He came once, and He will come again, to desire His Second Coming."

"Christians are called to renew their hope in the definitive coming of the Kingdom of God, preparing for it daily in their hearts . . ."

Pope John Paul II performed his role to perfection as the "spark," igniting the flame of a new evangelization, to prepare the world for the coming of the Kingdom of God. As his reward and also as a prophetic sign to the faithful, he was taken home on a First Saturday, a Fatima devotion, which, by providence, was on the eve of the Feast of Divine Mercy. In Manila, it was three o'clock on the morning of the feast itself. St. Faustina was surely waiting at the gates of Paradise to welcome His Holiness on her Feast Day.

In 2004, the year before he left us, Pope John Paul received 12 personal messages from Jesus, dictated to Anne, the third Servant in our story, a housewife and mother, whom her bishop describes as "a wife and mother of small children who is devoted to her husband and family. I know her to be a deeply spiritual and committed person."

A few days after receiving the personal messages, His Holiness received Anne's emissaries in a private audience. A few months later, Anne and her husband were asked to travel to Rome, where they met with the close personal friend of His Holiness who had delivered the messages to him.

Anne's role, obviously, is to continue the work begun by St. Faustina and continued by Pope John Paul II: to prepare mankind for Jesus' return. And this story, amazing as it is, could end here. But on September 27, 2005, Anne received by interior locution a message from St. Faustina. She said on September 27, 2005:

"Anne, our missions are destined to be joined. Your mission is an extension of my mission in that it is all part of the Divine Mercy. Jesus has put a great amount of graces in the pot that is the Volumes. Regardless of how many souls dip their cups into this pot, they will come up filled with graces because the Lord has willed that the amount be limitless. It is the same with the mission Our Lord entrusted to my soul. Will Jesus come to a point where He stops granting graces of mercy for the world because He has granted enough? This is impossible. Jesus does not limit His mercy for the world. Nor does He limit the conversion graces attached to your mission. You have my personal commitment to assist you in this project, and in every project. It is good that you have come to know me, Anne, because you know that I understand your struggles. You can trust my advice in every situation."

This first message was followed by a series of messages. This connection stirred Anne's desire to visit the Mother House of St. Faustina in Poland. And as Providence would have it, Sister Briege McKenna and Fr. Kevin Scallon called in September, 2005 to invite her to join them on a trip to Poland to visit the birthplace of Pope John Paul II and the Convent of the Sisters of Our Lady of Mercy where St. Faustina had lived.

This is Sister Briege's account of their visit to Poland:

"On the second day of a pilgrimage to the Divine Mercy Shrine in Cracow Lagiewniki, I attended Mass celebrated by Fr. Kevin Scallon in the convent chapel. In the afternoon of that day we visited the sisters' convent, thanks to the kindness of Fr. Tadeusz Skrzypczyk who knew the Mother Superior very well. Anne was with us on this occasion so we decided to introduce her to the Mother Superior. We explained to the sisters who Anne was and spoke about the messages and her writings. Anne then began to tell the sisters about her experiences with the Lord and most recently with St. Faustina herself. When she mentioned that her mission was to spread the message of Jesus Christ the Returning King, the Mother Superior told her about something very strange that had happened to her the day before. She explained that on her feast day an artist friend of hers had presented her with a painting, which he had told Mother Superior would be a painting of her patron saint. However when he gave her the painting, he explained that it was a painting of Christ the King. She immediately went off to fetch the painting and when we saw it, all of us in the room were amazed and recognized that this painting was to be the authentic image for the apostolate representing Jesus Christ the Returning King. It was obvious that the Mother Superior had the exact same sense, because she immediately presented the painting to Anne telling her that she was certain that it was really meant for Anne. We all felt that we were present at a moment of great significance which we will look back on with gratitude.

"In the days before coming to Poland, Anne shared with me that she had received messages from St. Faustina who told her that the revelation of Divine Mercy and of Jesus Christ the Returning King were intimately connected which is why she was so amazed to receive the painting; almost, you might say, from the hands of St. Faustina herself. St. Faustina had told her that the Divine Mercy devotion was more for these times in which we live than for any other time in the past.

"For myself, I feel very convinced of the authenticity of the messages which Anne has shared with the world through her writings and I look forward to the book which she has written. The great consolation I take from all of this is that the Lord is visibly purifying the world and the Church, and that please God, all us will live to see the new springtime which will emerge from these times of purification."

Anne's journal entry adds:

"That morning, St. Faustina told me in a locution that she intended to link our missions. I did not know how she would do that but she did it through the picture. Father Kevin and Sister Briege stated that as Faustina had the image of The Divine Mercy, the Returning King is the image for our mission."

So, this is the amazing story of how the Lay Apostles of Jesus Christ the Returning King received from St. Faustina, as it were, its official portrait of the Savior King. But this story does not end here.

Anne continues:

"We then left and went to a church called Calgary. Pope John Paul II reportedly loved it and came there on pilgrimage with his father. It was another extraordinary place. We left there and went to John Paul II's place of birth, an apartment in Wadowice. I was very moved because he had such difficulties in that he also lost his mother young, as well as a brother, and later his father. Good heavens, Jesus was jealous of his little heart and prepared him well through suffering. It moved me to no end. I looked at a picture of him as a young man. I am carrying such a heartache of loneliness for Jesus.

I said, "Holy Father, I missed you in Rome." (He was admitted to the hospital the day my husband and I arrived with Archbishop Hannan.)

The Holy Father began to speak and said this:

"You must be brave. You will need courage, but it will be provided for you from heaven. I will help you in many ways, little Anne. I wanted to see you in Rome but it was not His will. You were holy to accept this so peacefully. . . . Anne, you are a mother and your children are important. Do not worry so much for them because Jesus and Mary will protect them. You must work for your mission with total commitment to His will. We are helping in each detail. You saw that today when St. Faustina gave you the picture of our King. Anne, there are no coincidences when it comes to this mission. Understand that you have only to ask for what you need and it will come to you."

Anne: "Well, I did ask for many things for the mission. I love this man. I am grateful he spoke to me and he told me he will speak to me again tomorrow. Praise Jesus who spoils me with graces and blessings."

A series of messages was given by St. Faustina to Anne.

"*The image of Jesus Christ the Returning King should be spread throughout the world. There are many graces attached to this image. Like the image of The Divine Mercy, this image of Christ will be widely recognized as a source of goodness and healing. All who venerate this image will be blessed. I am grateful that God allows me the privilege of assisting in this mission. Each apostle should feel the same way and each apostle should thank God for being chosen to serve. Such joy flows from heaven. Bask in the joy, dear apostles, because your King is returning.*"

On November 9, 2005, St. Faustina said:

"*Dear friends of Jesus, heed our words. The time for Divine*"

Mercy to flow into the world has come. Any soul who cooperates with heaven in this project will experience this mercy in his own soul first, because God's mercy flows through the one who requests it and then out into the world. You will be the first recipient of this fragrant heavenly gift and your soul will reflect the graces that have passed through it. How pleasing this makes you to Jesus. How you stand out as a friend of the Returning King. From heaven, we watch His apostles multiply and we count these souls as our friends. We feel great joy as so many make their way up the mountain of holiness. Many have climbed these paths before you and many will assist you. No apostle climbs alone. Be joyful in this time and join heaven as we beseech God for mercy for the whole world."*

The passing of the torch is now completed. This amazing story continues in our own lives as we face the coming trials and changes in the world that will prepare mankind for the New Time when justice, peace and love will reign with the Savior King.

Archbishop Rosales of Manila blesses the Volumes
with Howard Dee, on September 8, 2005.

Fr. Kevin Scallon, Anne, a lay apostle, Sr. Briege McKenna
and Fr. Tadeusz Skzypczyk with the sisters
in Cracow-Lagiewniki, Poland in October, 2005.

Fr. Kevin and Sr. Briege holding the painting.

The Lay Apostolate of Jesus Christ the Returning King:
A Theological Commentary
by Dr. Mark Miravalle

The following is an edited, transcribed version of a talk given by Dr. Mark Miravalle, Professor of Theology and Mariology at the Franciscan University of Steubenville, in presentation of a theological commentary on the messages of Anne, the Lay Apostolate of Jesus Christ the Returning King, and the present position of the Catholic Church on these messages. The presentation was delivered at the Eucharistic Day of Renewal, Tinley Park, Illinois, February 10, 2007.

I would like to begin with a quote from the preface to the definitive Church commentary written by Pope Benedict XIV (while Cardinal Lambertini) in the 18th century on the nature and efficacy of authentic private relation within the Church's history and life:

"The Church began with miracles and divine gifts, and being one she continues the same. As the ancient dispensation began with Moses, and was inaugurated with miracles, so it continued from age to age, to the pond of Probatica, (cf. Jn. 5:2). The dispensation of the gospel is more glorious than that of the law, (2 Cor. 3:9) and is fulfilled in measure beyond the capacity of its predecessor... If the miracles of the law ceased not at the death of Moses, and if the record of them is not confined to the Pentateuch, but is continued through the history of kings and prophets, much more are we to expect a similar result in the history of Holy Church. The Acts of the Apostles do but carry on the miraculous record of the Four Gospels; and is there any reason that we should suppose that marvelous gifts, graces, and miracles ceased with the apostolic age? This would be the reasoning of the Sadducees, who confined themselves to the five books of Moses, and disowned the prophets. They had closed their hearts against the perpetual evidence of their temple, and refused to believe in the interference of God, and His dealings with that economy under which they were living."

—Preface, Benedict XIV, On Heroic Virtue

These words testify to the ongoing existence and benefit of authentic private revelation throughout the history of the Church from its origins. This is why the Church, while understandably prudent in its caution, has also always remained open to the possibility of prophetic lights assisting the Church in its journey towards Christian holiness.

In specific reference to the messages of Anne which constitute the foundation for the Lay Apostolate of Jesus Christ the Returning King, I would like to offer a theological commentary on, firstly, what the Church looks at when, for example, a bishop deems it necessary to establish a commission to investigate a reported private revelation; and then, secondly, to apply these same Church criteria for authenticity to the message and mission received by Anne of the Lay Apostolate of Jesus Christ the Returning King. The Church offers us certain criteria by which we examine, "Is this reported revelation of God?" "Is it not of God?" The criteria used by the Church are fundamentally threefold:

Number one: Is the reported message in conformity with the

faith and moral teaching of the Catholic Church? In fact, Pope Benedict XIV said this must always be the first element you examine. Why? Because the Holy Spirit is not going to contradict Himself. The Holy Spirit is not going to speak the Truth of Jesus through the Magisterium and at the same time say something contradictory through an individual. So it is the Public Revelation contained in Scripture and Tradition, as interpreted by the Magisterium, that becomes the foundation to evaluate any reported private revelation. That's always the first place we look. Is the message according to the teachings of the Church?

Number two: The Church examines the phenomena, the nature of how things are reportedly received and any other concurring extraordinary reported events. Do these reported phenomena fit within the precedence of authentic Catholic spiritual and mystical tradition?

Number three: The Church looks at the spiritual fruits. Are there lasting conversions, and returns to the Faith and to the prayer and sacramental life of the Church? Are people returning to their vocations? Is there a peace of heart that was not there before the reported event that perdures, that lasts?

So using these three criteria of the Church for authenticity, let me briefly comment on what Anne reports to receive from Jesus, from God the Father, from the Blessed Mother, and from a variety of the saints and the angels.

The Message

What is the heart of this message of the Lay Apostolate of Jesus Christ the Returning King? The heart of the message calls to open our hearts to the extraordinary graces offered to us by Jesus in preparation for, and participation in, a profound spiritual coming and renewal of the presence of Jesus into our hearts that will prepare each person for some form of a dynamic public manifestation of Jesus Christ the Returning King.

What does that mean? It means there are at least two aspects concerning the Return of Jesus Christ in the message being reported: an ongoing entry of Jesus Christ into our hearts with new, generous, some would even say phenomenal, levels of spiritual generosity; and, secondly, some form of a public manifestation of Jesus Christ, the Returning King.

Now, we must immediately distinguish what Anne has received from Jesus as entirely distinct from two other erroneous concepts. First of all, there is no element in Anne's messages regarding any immediate end of the world with Jesus' final coming at any moment. This is simply not present in any of her messages.

Secondly, there is no trace in Anne's message of what the Church has identified as the heresy of millenarianism. What is the heresy of millenarianism? This was the early Church concept that Jesus was going to come back to the earth physically in His resurrected body; sit on a throne and definitively establish His heavenly Kingdom in this life, typically thought to be for a thousand year period (hence, the name millenarianism, from "millennium"—one thousand); that He was going to raise the bodies of the saints and bring them back to life in this life; and that Jesus and the saints were going to defeat the powers of darkness in this life, and therefore set up a heaven on earth in this life. All of this is condemned. That will not take place. Jesus will not come back in His resurrected body and establish an earthly kingdom with Him reigning for a thousand years in this life. Once again, after a thorough reading of the messages, there is not a trace of the heresy of millenarianism in these messages.

What does it bespeak? It bespeaks, once again, a dynamic, powerful return of Jesus Christ in our age spiritually, in our hearts, which could include some type of public manifestation, in an ongoing preparation of heart for His eventual physical coming. And coupled with that part of the message is an invitation to each one of us—an invitation to prepare, as Jesus wants us to be prepared for this dynamic coming in our time.

Now, this message of Anne is very complementary with several other authentic spiritual movements presently within the Church. For example, we have the profound spiritual prayer of Blessed John XXIII at the Second Vatican Council for a "new Pentecost" for our present age. Essentially, this Holy Father rightly believed the world needs a new descent of the Holy Spirit in our troubled age. Now that's the Vicar of Jesus on earth, in front of the fathers of an ecumenical council, saying that we need a renewed presence of the Holy Spirit today.

Anne's message is also complementary to the heavenly words of Our Lady of Fatima, said on July 13, 1917: "In the end, My Immaculate Heart will triumph and a period of peace will be given to the world." We can't have a period of peace externally, until there is a newfound peace internally, spiritually. That only comes with the peace of Jesus Christ.

The message is also similar to the ongoing theme of John Paul the Great in his call for a "New Springtime" for the Church. And I believe he made it very clear that we are not there yet. That's why one of his last books was called "Crossing the Threshold of Hope". We're not there yet. Persevere. There is a time of grace coming. There's better times ahead. But we're not there yet.

It is also interesting that some of the Fathers of the Church taught that there would be a type of "Temporal" or "Middle" Coming of Jesus. The first coming of Jesus is, of course, His coming as an infant at the Incarnation. The last coming of Jesus takes place at the end of time with the end of the world. But several Fathers believed there would also be a middle coming of Jesus between the other comings where Jesus would come in His "Spirit." And His Spirit, along with Jesus, would renew the earth and a period of peace would be granted to humanity. After a time of conflict, a period of peace will come.

These are all contemporary and congruent messages with what Anne has received from Jesus. A coming of Jesus Christ, spiritual and dynamic, that calls for our preparation, and calls for our assistance.

The Five Duties of The Lay Apostle

Now along with this central aspect of the message, there are more specifically the five duties which Jesus is asking of his lay apostles. Again, I would like to offer a brief theological commentary on these five duties, which are for all those interested in helping to prepare and to fully benefit from this coming of Jesus which He invites us to participate in.

The first duty is the daily praying of the Allegiance Prayer, the Morning Offering, and a brief prayer for the Holy Father. What is the Allegiance Prayer? The Allegiance Prayer, as received by Anne, is the following prayer:

> *"Dear God in heaven, I pledge my allegiance to You. I give You my life, my work and my heart. In turn, give me the grace of obeying Your every direction to the fullest possible extent."*

My friends, what is intrinsic to this message is a new generosity of grace for those who are willing to receive it, on a daily basis; and even on a momentary basis. The second part of the prayer can easily be under appreciated as to its profound significance: "…in turn, give me the grace of obeying Your every direction to the fullest possible extent." That translates into asking Jesus to give us the ability of listening to and obeying His constant, ongoing directions for our lives, directions that He truly gives us at every moment. But this requires our constant listening, our consistent docility and obedience to these ongoing directions of the heart. It is like asking Jesus, not only by the day, but by the hour, and by the moment, "How do You wish me to serve You, Lord?" "Jesus, how do You wish me to reflect You now?" So this Allegiance Prayer is really saying, I give myself to God—life, work, heart—please give my every daily action. What else can you give to Jesus beyond that?

And in return, Jesus will give to us what we need each day. It is to ask: "Jesus, help me to know what I should say to my spouse, right now, who is in trial? Jesus, what should I be saying to my child? What about my friend who has called me in distress? What about my situation at work? I need You to direct me at these times. I need You to direct me at all times." And He is saying: "I will, if you let Me." This is the Allegiance Prayer.

This Allegiance Prayer is then coupled with the Morning Offering. The Morning Offering is the traditional prayer where we give Jesus, through the Immaculate Heart of Mary, our prayers, works, joys, and sufferings for the intentions of the Sacred Heart, in union with the Holy Sacrifice of the Mass, and in reparation for our sins. Again, dear friends, do not miss the profundity of what is contained in this prayer.

Jesus is saying that He wants us to enter the greatest thing He has ever accomplished: the work of Redemption. It is as if Jesus is saying to us through this prayer: "I merited the graces on Calvary, and secondarily My Mother with Me, and I give you the opportunity to release these graces. And how do you do that? By offering everything of every day to Me: your prayers, works, joys (which you often times forget to offer) and your sufferings."

What happens theologically and spiritually is that these offerings of ours allow Jesus to release, from the storehouses of graces which He already merited superabundantly, graces to be applied to your husband, or to your wife, or to your child, or to your friend, or to complete strangers in another part of the world. How many people will die before our day is over today? And yet Jesus knows every grace they need at the moment of their death, and that can come from right here at this conference hall, if we give it to Him. That's being a co-worker, a co-redeemer. That's what St. Paul says in Colossians 1:24, that we are called to "make up what is lacking in the sufferings of Christ for the sake of His body which is the Church." That means we offer our sacrifices and joys, so that His grace can enter the world in a powerful way. But He also says to do this, we, (and I especially think this is true of those of us in the western world), we are going to have to "slow down".

Here, let me read to you His direct words, which were revealed to Anne on August 9, 2005. He says:

"My children, why do you hurry so? Why do you feel you must move so quickly through your days? This is not the way I intended the children of God to live. You may tell Me that you have many things to do. I respond to you by say-

ing that you are trying to do too much. You will not be holy if you move so quickly. I want My beloved apostles to move slowly and thoughtfully through their days. I want you to make decisions on what I am asking you to do and what you are busying yourself with that is not from Me. I want your way of life to change and I am asking you to make this change now."

All of this is part of what He calls his "Rescue Mission". Essentially, this is not new to the Church. In fact, in 1943, Pope Pius XII wrote an encyclical on the Church entitled, Mystici Corporis, "On The Mystical Body of Jesus Christ." The major thrust of this document on the Church was this: We are one mystical body. If you pray for someone, if you do a virtuous act, it affects someone else in the Body. And if you do something wrong, it doesn't just hurt you, it also hurts someone else in the Body.

Parenthetically, I find it fascinating that we understand this principle clearly as applied to sports, but many have lost its meaning as regards to the Church. For example, imagine in a football game if the right guard jumps off sides. The referee doesn't say, "Alright, number 78, you go 5 yards back." The whole team goes back. Or the receiver makes a nice one-handed catch in the end zone. They don't put his name up on the scoreboard with six points; the whole team gets six points. Why? Because it is a team effort.

So is our Church. So is this Rescue Mission for all humanity. We are supposed to do this together as a team. That means your sufferings, your chores done out of love, your patience with a family member, all becomes an opportunity for supernatural graces for you, for your family, or for somebody on the other side of the planet. And Jesus, in this message, is saying that He wants you to join this team, to take this call of the Rescue Mission and to incorporate it today. So, it's not a new call, but it's rather a renewed Catholic call of saving souls with Jesus.

Quite frankly, it's the opportunity for which the angels envy us! St. Thomas Aquinas rightly taught that the angels are superior to us in every created way, except they can't physically suffer with Jesus. But you and I can suffer with Jesus. In fact, we can do something even more remarkable. We can take the suffering for which we have no control over anyway and we can transform it, through our patient and obedient acceptance and endurance, into a supernatural release of grace for our salvation, for someone else's salvation, and now in preparation for Jesus' new, dynamic coming into our time, in whatever form that takes. This is the call of living our Morning Offering as part of our first duty as lay apostles.

The second duty of the lay apostle is a weekly hour of Eucharistic Adoration. Quite simply, there is no way we can consistently participate in this type of Rescue Mission for souls unless He feeds us; unless He fills us; for the world, and our family, and everything in between, will suck our efforts out of us. His promise is, You come before Me for an hour before the Blessed Sacrament, and I will fill you, I will give you the graces, no matter how much is taken from you. And so, a Eucharistic Hour once a week is the second duty of the lay apostle.

The third duty of the lay apostle is a monthly gathering with other lay apostles. Here the Luminous Mysteries will be prayed and the monthly message which is given on the first of every month to Anne will be read and meditated upon. Then follows a time of fellowship. This means you get with other lay apostles, you pray, you listen, and then you share your hearts. I don't know about you, but sometimes I am more encouraged by hearing about the sufferings, the challenges, and the failures of others, rather than just by hearing about the successes, the trophies, and the victories of others. There is a certain consolation in knowing that we all have trials and crosses, and we are called to help and encourage each other to carry our own respective crosses. It can also console our fellow lay apostle when we have the humility to share our own weakness that, "I'm having a tough time at home. I'm barely making it at work. I'm really battling depression. I'm having a tough time dealing with my children, who are out of the faith, etc, etc." That's part of what the gathering is. We help each other persevere and continue in this Renewal, to continue for this mission.

The fourth duty of the lay apostle is monthly Confession. This used to be the old pastoral rule of thumb. When you asked a priest, "Look, I'm serious about Christian holiness. How often should I go to Confession?" the standard spiritual advice was, "About once a month." Why? Does that mean we fall in to mortal sin once a month? No, not necessarily. It means we want to meet the Divine Physician once a month. We want to enter what St. Augustine called "the medicine box" once a month and be healed. And at least once a month, we want to get graces specifically to assist us in our particular areas of sin and weakness. Maybe it's regarding the sins we've been battling for the last 20 to 30 years—we've all got types of sins that seem to hang on to us, habits of sin that are so difficult to break. That's what the grace of the confessional is for. Not only are your sins forgiven, but you get graces that are specific to overcoming your particular sins. That is why there is a monthly sacramental call for this extraordinary opportunity of reconciling and healing grace.

The fifth duty of the lay apostle is to follow the example of Jesus Christ as found in Scripture, treating all others with His patience and kindness. Once again, in humility, we must start with the admittance that we cannot do this alone. We can't live the life of Jesus in patience and kindness unless He fills us with the grace to do so. This is also why a critical part of His message is a call to, at least once a day, reserve a time of silence for Him, some period of silence every day where He, once again, can replenish us; when He can instruct us; where He can inspire us. The world takes it from us; He returns it to us in overflowing abundance. His generosity is a hundredfold for what we do, and for what is taken from us. But, we have to give Him the time each day to restore us in the mission.

There are also consistent references in the messages to the powerful maternal presence and intercession of our Blessed Mother. She is the Mediatrix of all graces. Her generosity, her ability in heaven, in purgatory, and for us, the pilgrim Church on earth, is unequalled, second only to that of her Divine Son. We must go to the Blessed Mother; we must use her great weapon of the Rosary against the Adversary; we must consecrate ourselves to Her Sorrowful and Immaculate Heart.

Along with Our Lady is the call to invoke the efficacious intercession of the angels and saints. One profound maxim that issues forth from these messages is: Heaven is at our disposal. What does that mean? It means the angels and the saints, during this time which Jesus calls a period of disobedience, have been given special intercessory power on our behalf. Jesus wishes to initiate a period of obedience upon the world, but to do that He needs our help, and He is giving the saints and the angels accentuated intercessory power to aid us. This help of the angels and saints is more generous, arguably, than any other time in history, because Jesus knows our struggles in this dark age of disobedience.

This call refers to our guardian angels, to our patron saints, and to the great number of the saints that have specifically revealed, through Anne, about their former walks in life, their challenges while on earth, and how they can help us. So, we're not in this alone. We have extraordinary intercessory power from our great friends in the Mystical Body, the angels and the saints.

So, in sum, the first criterion which the Church looks at regarding a private revelation is the message, and in the messages received by Anne, there is absolutely no doctrinal error to be found. Quite the contrary, the message is doctrinally orthodox, in line with the teachings of the Papal Magisterium, and sublimely inspiring in the heart of Catholic Tradition.

Phenomena and Publications

The second criterion of what the Church looks at in determining authenticity is the phenomena. The phenomena deal with any types of reported supernatural experiences that surround the event, as well as the various modes in which the messages are received.

Anne describes two principal modes of how she receives these messages. The first mode of transmission is through interior vision. After Jesus brings her "into Himself" in prayer, as Anne describes it, it is at that time, during that time of mystical union between herself and Jesus, that Jesus either gives her a vision, reveals a message to her, or in some cases can bring her to a spiritual location or a spiritual state for the sake of having Anne document what she experiences.

This process is classic in the mystical tradition of the Church in that the union, the intimacy with Jesus, is what becomes the foundation for the spiritual communication of what is later revealed. This communication is typically not just for the individual, but either for a group of people, in some cases, or for all of humanity.

Interior vision is the first mode of what Anne receives, which is sometimes coupled with what is in classical theology called "mystical transports". Anne has been brought to heaven, and she has explained and described the experience there. She has also been brought to purgatory and has described her experiences there.

The second principle mode of what she receives is through locutions. A locution is where a person will hear words, not audibly with the ears, but interiorly with the heart. They hear the words clearly in this mode, not as just an inspiration, nor merely a new insight, but specific words audible to the soul that can be recorded in dictational form.

These messages, both the interior visions, and the locutions, under these different phenomenal modes of communication, are recorded in a series of small Volumes and shorter booklets. Allow me to briefly mention the themes that are present, because it manifests Jesus' instruction and loving concern for us in our contemporary situations of the 21st Century.

The Volumes

The themes contained in the short books designated as "The Volumes" are the following:

Volume One: *Thoughts on Spirituality*

Volume Two: *Conversations with the Eucharistic Heart of Jesus*

Volume Three: *God the Father Speaks to His Children; The Blessed Mother Speaks to Her Bishops and Priests*

Volume Four: *Jesus the King; Heaven Speaks to Priests; Jesus Speaks to Sinners*

Volume Six: *Heaven Speaks to Families.* (I must recommend Volume Six in a special way to those who know the domestic challenges of raising kids today. I've got eight children myself. It's always a battle against domestic chaos. That's part of family life today. The words that Jesus, Our Blessed Mother, and St. Joseph give to families are pure super-natural wisdom.

I especially have to underscore the inspired counsel of St. Joseph, as he instructs fathers in this tragically "fatherless" generation. In an age where fathers have, in many cases, identity crises, St. Joseph talks about our role as being a firm, but present force in the family. We are not first to be a disciplinarian, not first. First, we are to provide a gentle presence of guidance, love and protection. The entire Volume contains tremendous messages for the family that could be read commonly by the family).

Volume Seven: *Greetings from Heaven.* These are individual messages from the saints. In a beautiful way, the saints share their struggles on earth and why they have been given the graces to help us particularly in their own previous area of struggle.

Volume Nine: *Angels.* The power of the angels, the disposition of the angels, how you have a spiritual person given to you, higher on the created level, more intelligent, waiting to assist you and guide you towards heaven, requiring only that you ask.

Volume Ten: *Jesus Speaks to His Apostles.* This Volume represents an overall exhortation to the lay apostles.

Volumes Five and Eight have been recorded, but have not yet been published and distributed.

Books

There are also the two major books at present. *Climbing the Mountain* speaks about Anne's experiences in heaven. *The Mist of Mercy* describes Anne's experiences of purgatory. For those who battle with fear of purgatory, I strongly recommend this work, as you will experientially receive the teachings of the Church, that in purgatory there is always Christian faith, hope and charity. There is no backdoor of purgatory to hell.

This account reflects the authentic Catholic understanding of purgatory as being a true experience of mercy while at the same time accomplishing the purification that we may need, and, if so, would actually desire before entrance into heaven.

Heaven Speaks Booklet Series

There are twenty themes in these smaller series of messages called the "Heaven Speaks" messages (some of which are also contained in the books).

The first set of ten "Heaven Speaks" series of messages discuss the following topics: Abortion, Addictions, Victims of Clerical Abuse, Consecrated Souls, Depression, Divorce, Prisoners, Soldiers, Stress, and Young Adults.

In the second set of ten series, just published and released at this conference, the topics address: Those Considering Suicide, Those Who Are Away from the Church, Those Who Are Dying, Those Who Do Not Know Jesus, Those Who Experience Tragedy, Those Who Fear Purgatory, Those Who Have Rejected God, Those Who Struggle to Forgive, Those Who Struggle from Financial Need, and Parents Who Worry About Their Children's Salvation.

My friends, Jesus knows our own struggles right now. In my own research and experience with the major private revelations historically, and within the last fifty years, the authentic messages that Jesus and Our Blessed Mother have given during the 1970s, 1980s, and 1990s, were dealing to a large degree with the fact that we had to be shaken from laxity and complacency. We were not taking seriously the Christian life. The world had really absorbed us.

In my opinion, Jesus knows that He is now talking to generation that to a prominent degree is wounded, and therefore He firstly has to heal us, He has to balm us, He has to repair us, so that we can then be part in this Rescue Mission for souls. And that's what I find to be a particular grace within these messages. They are consoling. There's a love, there's gentleness, there's a compassion that makes us want to join in the Rescue Mission for souls, firstly out of love for Him. Even though we are not comparing Jesus with Jesus or Mary with Mary within the domain of their authentic messages to the world. But it's a highlight; it's an accentuation of these messages. He knows our needs today and He wants to bring us those healing graces, and then He wants to enable us, in the same process, to be able to bring these graces to those around us at the same time.

Fruits and Testimonies

The third general criterion of the Church is the criterion of spiritual fruits. Now, in a very short period of time, with these messages having been revealed initially in 2003, the publication of these messages starting in December 2003, and distribution in January 2004, these messages have covered the four corners of the earth, and with them have come a myriad of international testimonies of conversion, faith, reconciliation, and spiritual peace. The messages are being translated into every major language, and they are presently in the process of being translated into Mandarin and being brought into China. The spiritual fruits have been nothing short of ubiquitous, and in such a brief time span of promulgation.

As just one example, Anne came and spoke at the Franciscan University of Steubenville at the invitation of Fr. Michael Scanlan, the former President and present Chancellor of Franciscan University. Fr. Michael mentioned to me recently that since Anne spoke in October, there hasn't been a day when a student or faculty member has not come up to him and said, "Thanks, Fr. Mike for letting Anne come—it's changed my life." The University now has a lay apostolate meeting each month in the University Chapel. These graces are spreading in similar fashion throughout the world.

There have also been a number of Catholic leaders who have embraced this message in faith and joy of heart, and have become principal distributors in their respective countries and regions. People like Fr. Michael Scanlan; Fr. Francis Martin, the renowned Scripture scholar from the Washington, D.C. region; Sr. Briege McKenna and Fr. Kevin Scallon from Ireland; and Ambassador Howard Dee from the Philippines. Ambassador Howard Dee was the former Vatican Ambassador to the Holy See for the Philippines under the pontificate of John Paul II. John Paul II used to call Howard, "Our Lady's Ambassador," because every time they talked together they spoke about the Blessed Mother. It was, in fact, through Howard Dee that I came to read these messages.

And I must confess that I had to be somewhat providentially "cornered" to do so. I was returning from a conference where I had given a talk to approximately 100 priests outside of Milan, and my assistant had given me my plane ticket which should have been scheduled to depart for home on Sunday morning. It was a 250.00 dollar cab ride from the conference site to the Milan Airport and when I arrived at the Milan Airport and handed my airline ticket to the attendant, she said, "I am sorry, sir, but this ticket is for departure on Monday morning." I took that unfortunate news without the least bit of any appreciation for redemptive suffering.

I soon located a chapel in the Milan airport, with a Eucharistic chapel present. Ambassador Dee had sent me four Volumes of Anne's messages some three months earlier, which I had ignored for three months and had thrown into my briefcase. And so, cornered in the Milan Airport, I thought, what else shall I do? I'll give these Volumes a brief look.

I proceeded to spend the next 18 of the 22 hours of my wait in that chapel reading these messages before the Blessed Sacrament. After the first hours of reading with my heart afire from these messages, my only fear was that my flight would leave before I could finish the Volumes. Personally, (and again my personal testimony is least important), it was a life-changing event that I will always thank Jesus for, and thank Him as well for the great spiritual benefit they have been for my wife and children, who have all heard and embraced these messages.

Present Position of the Church

What then is the present position of the Church regarding Anne and the Lay Apostolate? I had the particular privilege of meeting with Anne's bishop in the diocese of Kilmore in

Ireland. Bishop Leo O'Reilly is a humble, and in my opinion, a holy man. He is a man whose heart is entirely at one with the Church. He has personally read the messages and he conveyed to me in our meeting in Ireland his trust and confidence, which has led to his granting permission to distribute these messages. Bishop O'Reilly has also met with the Congregation for the Doctrine of the Faith. Every single message has been submitted to the Congregation for the Doctrine of the Faith, the Vatican Commission that examines private revelation, and the Congregation has responded that it is satisfied with the process of how Bishop O'Reilly has handled this event to the present point. Therefore, there is no more that could be done in the order of Church obedience and loyalty with regards to these messages.

In conclusion, using the very criteria designated by the Church in cases of reported revelation, I can personally state that the message is sound. The phenomena can be found in the heart of the Church's mystical tradition. And the spiritual fruits are internationally documentable and supraabundant. This revelation possesses all the classic characteristics of supernatural authenticity.

The Church allows us to make a personal acceptance of these messages, even before there's any type of official approval. You will remember that Jacinta and Francisco were beatified for living the Fatima messages approximately eight years before the Fatima messages were approved. That's the Holy Spirit. And that's the freedom the Church gives with prudence. So I want to end with one of the messages that Jesus gave, because hopefully He won't have to corner you as He cornered me. Hopefully today you will take the opportunity to read this message because He is calling you to this mission.

I end with the words of Jesus, revealed on June 1, 2005:

"My brothers and sisters, how I love you. How eager I am that you use the graces available to you. When a soul understands this mission and begins to ask for graces for others, heaven is joyful. In the same way, those on earth who are interceded for begin to benefit and change. Grace surrounds them. Their souls become alert because there is hope. Dear ones, help Me. I want every soul to return to Me. I am waiting for each soul to become open so My graces can flood that soul. Many of you have seen this and you understand. For those of you who have not seen this happen, please, ask Me for graces for a soul who is far from Me. Continue asking Me. Ask Me for graces for strangers. I will come to them in a special way. I will observe them closely as only I can, given My knowledge of them, and I will find the perfect moment. While I wait for this moment I will be allowing them to benefit from your prayers and wishes by sending moments of grace and people of grace into their lives. Think, My friends. Did I not do this for you at sometime in your life? Did I not pursue you when I knew you were far away? If you were never far away perhaps I encouraged you if you felt abandoned or afraid. I have graces for each soul in darkness. Please, work for Me now and you will see souls returning. All is well, My dear friends. You are children of heaven. And as children of heaven, you have nothing to fear. There is only good possible for you. The earth is a temporary residence. Your home is in heaven, so when you come here, you

The Nourishment You Seek

By Sr. Briege McKenna, O.S.C.

I met Anne in early 2005 at the request of Archbishop Hannan, the former Archbishop of New Orleans. I was struck by her simplicity and above all by her desire not to be known in the public forum. She shared with me some of her concern about how she would circulate the *Volumes* which are called *Direction for Our Times*. There is something about Anne which makes it easy to believe what she tells you.

Against this background, I began to read the Volumes of directions given to her by the Lord. These writings have a quality about them which I have not encountered elsewhere. They remind me of Saint Faustina's *Diary* and also the revelations to St. Margaret Mary concerning *Devotion to the Sacred Heart*.

I suppose we should not be surprised that the Holy Trinity gives revelations of this kind to people like Anne. After all, it has been happening in the Church from the very beginning. Following on the revelation concerning devotion to the *Divine Mercy*, these little Volumes remind us again of the tenderness of the Father's love and the mercy of our Savior Jesus Christ. Many people who have read these Volumes are profoundly impressed and moved by what they read.

The Volumes begin with a series of teachings concerning basic spirituality, going into details which people will see as extremely wise and very, very helpful. The first Volume opens with *Thoughts on Spirituality*. Other Volumes include the *Eucharistic Heart of Jesus*, the *Father Speaking to His Children*, the *Blessed Virgin Addressing Priests, Bishops and*

Religious, and even a Volume on the *Angels.* There is a directness about the writing which expresses at one and the same time great love and the promise of unique graces which the Lord wants to give to everyone. There are many references to events and purification, all of which will be familiar to those who have read accounts of Fatima and Medjugorje. These events are intended to purify the human race, to renew the face of the earth and to usher in a time of triumphant grace for the Church throughout the world.

I find myself reading these Volumes and rereading them. They have provided me with an amazing degree of spiritual nourishment and interior blessing. To say that I recommend them to anyone would be an understatement. These little books in which the Lord speaks to us through his servant Anne have a relevance and an immediacy that is impossible to ignore.

Frequent Confession

By Father Bill McCarthy, M.S.A.

Carl Jung, the great psychologist, estimated that more than 95 percent of all Americans walk around loaded with sin, guilt, bitterness, and "unforgiveness." He said that it is the way the average person throughout the world lives. They pile on all the sin and guilt and "unforgiveness" of their childhood, their young adulthood, their twenties and their thirties, and try to enter a new day with peace, love and joy—the three great gifts of the Spirit. Obviously, they cannot do so. So often they settle for a quick fix of drugs, alcohol, promiscuity, sports, shopping, TV, and carnal living.

For thirty years, Carl Jung searched for an answer. When he was 84, God gave him the answer. One of his clients, he noticed, showed no signs of guilt or bitterness. He excitedly asked her why not. She mentioned that she was a practicing Catholic and that she believed that Jesus, by His death and resurrection, had suffered and died for her sins; and then on Easter Sunday evening, He gave the power to forgive sins to His priests by saying, "Receive the Holy Spirit. Whose sins you shall forgive, they are forgiven."

He looked at her with great amazement and said, "You've found the pearl of great price for which I've searched diligently for more than thirty years. Please never stop going to confession."

Karl Menninger, another great psychologist, who decried the fact that psychologists were denying sin, wrote the now famous book, "Whatever Happened to Sin?" He claimed that sin and guilt as well as bitterness were the most crippling emotions in the human soul.

Jesus is the greatest psychologist. He alone knows what the soul needs—a way to cleanse sin, guilt, bitterness, and hatred through His shed blood. That is why He said to His priests, "As the Father has sent me, I now send you." Then He breathed upon them and said, "Receive the Holy Spirit. Whose sins you shall forgive, they are forgiven."

Realizing the darkness that has overcome mankind and the culture of death to which mankind has descended, Pope John Paul II—this great apostle of mercy who had already beatified Sister Faustina—encouraged every baptized Catholic to go to confession frequently. It is in the Sacrament of Confession that three awesome, wondrous miracles of grace take place. First, every bit of sin and guilt is washed clean through the Blood of the Lamb administered through the absolution of the priest. Second, all bitterness, unjust anger and resentment are released. Third, the penitents are given the awesome power to completely forgive themselves and get on with their lives.

The late Holy Father stated:

"I am also asking for renewed pastoral courage in ensuring that the day-to-day teaching of Christian communities persuasively and effectively presents the practice of the Sacrament of Reconciliation. As you will recall, in 1984 I dealt with this subject in the Post-Synodal Exhortation Reconciliatio et Paenitentia, which synthesized the results of an Assembly of the Synod of Bishops devoted to this question. My invitation then was to make every effort to face the crisis of "the sense of sin" apparent in today's culture. But I was even more insistent in calling for a rediscovery of Christ as *mysterium pietatis*, the one in whom God shows us His compassionate heart and reconciles us fully with Himself. It is this face of Christ that must be rediscovered through the

Sacrament of Penance, which for the faithful is the ordinary way of obtaining forgiveness and the remission of serious sins committed after Baptism."

If you want to live a life with real joy, true peace of soul and awesome love, an integral part of the answer is frequent confession. The more you are cleansed of sin, guilt and unforgiveness, the more receptive your soul is for all the fruits of the Spirit.

Eucharist Adoration

By Anne, a lay apostle

The Real Presence of Our Lord Jesus Christ in the Eucharist is being challenged today. This should not surprise us. Through the Eucharist, Jesus sends graces and healing in a constant flow. The Eucharist is the Source of all goodness. Each Eucharistic chapel is like a heavenly porthole, through which comes light for a dark world. In these places of worship, heaven and earth are joined and our sweet, kind Jesus makes Himself available in a continuous way. This, to me, is the height of benevolence.

As lay apostles, we pledge to give Our Lord one hour of Eucharistic Adoration each week. For seasoned adorers, this is as natural as breathing. Those newer to the practice will no doubt wonder what they will do for a full hour in a chapel. There is no television, no radio, no talking. There is only Jesus Christ, fully present, in the humble Host. The first few minutes will possibly seem long, but shortly after, the time will fly.

One of my favorite experiences in Adoration is to listen to souls as they arrive and settle in. There is a small disruption in the silence as rosaries are located and books set aside. The soul shifts and fidgets a bit, getting comfortable in the chair or on the kneeler. The other adorers know it will take a minute or so and welcome the soul in their hearts. Soon there is silence again and all are free to reattach themselves to the heavenly breezes. After two or three minutes, you can hear the newly arrived soul begin to sigh. I know that souls are often unaware of their sighs. For me, these sighs are like music. The soul has connected to Christ. The body relaxes.

The Divine Healer has begun His work.

Another Adoration experience that delights me is to witness a soul who has fallen asleep. I know that we should stay awake with Jesus, but who among us has not drifted off? Jesus does not hold this against us. When I see or hear a soul sleeping, I praise God for the divine ministering that is occurring in the soul while the body rests.

I sometimes feel so distracted in prayer that I may as well be asleep. This no longer upsets me as I know that Jesus is working away in my soul, regardless of my struggles. I once apologized to Jesus and He said, "Be at peace. When your mind wanders, I go with you. It is good for Me to see where you go."

Jesus is welcome wherever I go. You may shudder, thinking of the darker meanderings of your mind. Don't. Just focus on Christ again. Jesus understands everything.

Often I arrive for Adoration in a bad mood. Perhaps I am tired, or unwell, or simply irritable that I am compelled to make this time for prayer when I have so many other things that seem more important. I am aware of the ridiculousness of that statement and yet I write it so that the reader will understand that all suffer temptations against prayer time. Nevertheless, I arrive. I have never, not once, left the chapel sorry that I spent time with Christ. Nor will you, my fellow apostle.

In a casual internet search, I encountered a statement that there are 6954 Eucharistic Adoration chapels in the United States and Canada. Praise God for each soul who made this number possible. You can access this list by going to **www.therealpresence.org**. This heavenly site even supplies maps, addresses, and phone numbers. Be faithful to Christ in this commitment to Eucharistic Adoration and He will change your life.

Always remember that the world changes one soul at a time. Begin with yours.

Appendix

Prayers Taken from The Volumes

Prayers to God the Father

"I trust You God. I offer You my pain in the spirit of acceptance and I will serve You in every circumstance."

"God my Father in heaven, You are all mercy. You love me and see my every sin. God, I call on You now as the Merciful Father. Forgive my every sin. Wash away the stains on my soul so that I may once again rest in complete innocence. I trust You, Father in heaven. I rely on You. I thank You. Amen."

"God my Father, calm my spirit and direct my path."

"God, I have made mistakes. I am sorry. I am Your child, though, and seek to be united to You."

"I believe in God. I believe Jesus is calling me. I believe my Blessed Mother has requested my help. Therefore I am going to pray on this day and every day."

"God my Father, help me to understand."

Prayers to Jesus

"Jesus, I give You my day."

"Jesus, how do You want to use me on this day? You have a willing servant in me, Jesus. Allow me to work for the Kingdom."

"Lord, what can I do today to prepare for Your coming? Direct me, Lord, and I will see to Your wishes."

"Jesus, how do You want to use me?"

"Lord, help me."

"Jesus, what do You think of all this? Jesus, what do You want me to do for this soul? Jesus, show me how to bring You into this situation."

"Jesus, love me."

Prayers to the Angels

"Angels from heaven, direct my path."

"Dearest angel guardian, I desire to serve Jesus by remaining at peace. Please obtain for me the graces necessary to maintain His divine peace in my heart."

Prayers for Children

"Jesus, forgive them."

"Mother Mary, help me to be good."

"God in heaven, You are the Creator of all things. Please send Your graces down upon our world."

"Jesus, I love You."

"Jesus, I offer You my day

How to Recite the Chaplet of Divine Mercy

The Chaplet of Mercy is recited using ordinary rosary beads of five decades. The Chaplet is preceded by two opening prayers from the *Diary* of Saint Faustina and followed by a closing prayer.

1. Make the Sign of the Cross

In the name of the Father, and of the Son, and of the Holy Spirit. Amen.

2. Optional Opening Prayers

You expired, Jesus, but the source of life gushed forth for souls, and the ocean of mercy opened up for the whole world. O Fount of Life, unfathomable Divine Mercy, envelop the whole world and empty Yourself out upon us.

O Blood and Water, which gushed forth from the Heart of Jesus as a fountain of mercy for us, I trust in You!

3. Our Father

Our Father, who art in heaven, hallowed be Thy name. Thy kingdom come; Thy will be done on earth as it is in heaven. Give us this day our daily bread; and forgive us our trespasses as we forgive those who trespass against us; and lead us not into temptation, but deliver us from evil. Amen.

4. Hail Mary

Hail Mary, full of grace. The Lord is with thee. Blessed art thou among women, and blessed is the fruit of thy womb, Jesus. Holy Mary, Mother of God, pray for us sinners, now and at the hour of our death. Amen.

5. The Apostles' Creed

I believe in God, the Father Almighty, Creator of Heaven and earth. I believe in Jesus Christ, His only Son, Our Lord. He was conceived by the power of the Holy Spirit and born of the Virgin Mary. He suffered under Pontius Pilate, was crucified, died, and

was buried. He descended to the dead. On the third day He rose
again. He ascended into Heaven, and is seated at the right hand of
the Father. He will come again to judge the living and the dead. I
believe in the Holy Spirit, the holy Catholic Church, the communion of saints, the forgiveness of sins, the resurrection of the
body, and the life everlasting. Amen.

6. The Eternal Father

Eternal Father, I offer You the Body and Blood, Soul and Divinity of Your Dearly Beloved Son, Our Lord, Jesus Christ, in atone-
ment for our sins and those of the whole world.

7. On the Ten Small Beads of Each Decade

For the sake of His sorrowful Passion, have mercy on us and on
the whole world.

8. Repeat for the remaining decades

Saying the "Eternal Father" (6) on the "Our Father" bead and then
10 "For the sake of His sorrowful Passion" (7) on the following
"Hail Mary" beads.

9. Conclude with Holy God

Holy God, Holy Mighty One, Holy Immortal One, have mercy on
us and on the whole world.

10. Optional Closing Prayer

Eternal God, in whom mercy is endless and the treasury of compassion—inexhaustible, look kindly upon us and increase Your
mercy in us, that in difficult moments we might not despair nor
become despondent, but with great confidence submit ourselves
to Your holy will, which is Love and Mercy itself.

To learn more about the image of The Divine Mercy, the Chaplet of Divine Mercy and the series of revelations given to St. Faustina Kowalska please contact:

Marians of the Immaculate Conception
Stockbridge, Massachusetts 01263
Telephone 800-462-7426
www.marian.org

How to Pray the Rosary

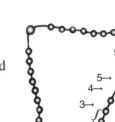

1. Make the Sign of the Cross and say the "Apostles Creed."
2. Say the "Our Father."
3. Say three "Hail Marys."
4. Say the "Glory be to the Father."
5. Announce the First Mystery; then say the "Our Father."
6. Say ten "Hail Marys," while meditating on the Mystery.
7. Say the "Glory be to the Father." After each decade say the following prayer requested by the Blessed Virgin Mary at Fatima: "O my Jesus, forgive us our sins, save us from the fires of hell, lead all souls to Heaven, especially those in most need of Thy mercy."
8. Announce the Second Mystery: then say the "Our Father." Repeat 6 and 7 and continue with the Third, Fourth, and Fifth Mysteries in the same manner.
9. Say the "Hail, Holy Queen" on the medal after the five decades are completed.

As a general rule, depending on the season, the Joyful Mysteries are said on Monday and Saturday; the Sorrowful Mysteries on Tuesday and Friday; the Glorious Mysteries on Wednesday and Sunday; and the Luminous Mysteries on Thursday.

Papal Reflections of the Mysteries

The Joyful Mysteries

The Joyful Mysteries are marked by the joy radiating from the event of the Incarnation. This is clear from the very first mystery, the Annunciation, where Gabriel's greeting to the Virgin of Nazareth is linked to an invitation to messianic joy: "Rejoice, Mary." The whole of salvation . . . had led up to this greeting.

(Prayed on Mondays and Saturdays, and optional on Sundays during Advent and the Christmas Season.)

The Luminous Mysteries

Moving on from the infancy and the hidden life in Nazareth to the public life of Jesus, our contemplation brings us to those mysteries which may be called in a special way "mysteries of light." Certainly, the whole mystery of Christ is a mystery of light. He is the "Light of the world" (John 8:12). Yet this truth emerges in a special way during the years of His public life. (Prayed on Thursdays.)

The Sorrowful Mysteries

The Gospels give great prominence to the Sorrowful Mysteries of Christ. From the beginning, Christian piety, especially during the Lenten devotion of the Way of the Cross, has focused on the individual moments of the Passion, realizing that here is found the culmination of the revelation of God's love and the source of our salvation. (Prayed on Tuesdays and Fridays, and optional on Sundays during Lent.)

The Glorious Mysteries

"The contemplation of Christ's face cannot stop at the image of the Crucified One. He is the Risen One!" The Rosary has always expressed this knowledge born of faith and invited the believer to pass beyond the darkness of the Passion in order to gaze upon Christ's glory in the Resurrection and Ascension. . . . Mary herself would be raised to that same glory in the Assumption. (Prayed on Wednesdays and Sundays.)

From the *Apostolic Letter The Rosary of the Virgin Mary*, Pope John Paul II, Oct. 16, 2002.

Prayers of the Rosary

The Sign of the Cross
In the name of the Father, and of the Son, and of the Holy Spirit. Amen.

The Apostles' Creed
I believe in God, the Father Almighty, Creator of heaven and earth. I believe in Jesus Christ, His only Son, Our Lord. He was conceived by the power of the Holy Spirit and born of the Virgin Mary. He suffered under Pontius Pilate, was crucified, died, and was buried. He descended to the dead. On the third day He rose again. He ascended into heaven, and is seated at the right hand of the Father. He will come again to judge the living and the dead. I believe in the Holy Spirit, the holy Catholic Church, the communion of saints, the forgiveness of sins, the resurrection of the body, and the life everlasting. Amen.

Our Father
Our Father, who art in heaven, hallowed be Thy name. Thy kingdom come; Thy will be done on earth as it is in heaven. Give us this day our daily bread; and forgive us our trespasses as we forgive those who trespass against us; and lead us not into temptation, but deliver us from evil. Amen.

Hail Mary
Hail Mary, full of grace. The Lord is with thee. Blessed art thou among women, and blessed is the fruit of thy womb, Jesus. Holy Mary, Mother of God, pray for us sinners, now and at the hour of our death. Amen.

Glory Be to the Father
Glory be to the Father, and to the Son, and to the Holy Spirit. As it was in the beginning, is now, and ever shall be, world without end. Amen.

Hail Holy Queen

Hail, Holy Queen, Mother of Mercy, our life, our sweetness and our hope, to thee do we cry, poor banished children of Eve; to thee do we send up our sighs, mourning and weeping in this vale of tears; turn, then, most gracious Advocate, thine eyes of mercy towards us, and after this, our exile, show unto us the blessed fruit of thy womb, Jesus. O clement, O loving, O sweet Virgin Mary!

Pray for us, O holy Mother of God, that we may be made worthy of the promises of Christ.

The Mysteries

First Joyful Mystery:
The Annunciation

And when the angel had come to her, he said, "Hail, full of grace, the Lord is with thee. Blessed art thou among women."

(Luke 1:28)

One *Our Father*, Ten *Hail Marys*,
One *Glory Be*, etc.

Fruit of the Mystery: ***Humility***

Second Joyful Mystery:
The Visitation

Elizabeth was filled with the Holy Spirit and cried out in a loud voice: "Blest are you among women and blest is the fruit of your womb." *(Luke* 1:41-42)

One *Our Father*, Ten *Hail Marys*,
One *Glory Be*, etc.

Fruit of the Mystery: ***Love of Neighbor***

Third Joyful Mystery:
The Birth of Jesus

She gave birth to her first-born Son and wrapped Him in swaddling clothes and laid Him in a manger, because there was no room for them in the place where travelers lodged.   (*Luke* 2:7)

One *Our Father*, Ten *Hail Marys*,
One *Glory Be*, etc.

Fruit of the Mystery: ***Poverty***

Fourth Joyful Mystery:
The Presentation

When the day came to purify them according to the law of Moses, the couple brought Him up to Jerusalem so that He could be presented to the Lord, for it is written in the law of the Lord, "Every first-born male shall be consecrated to the Lord."

(*Luke* 2:22-23)

One *Our Father*, Ten *Hail Marys*,
One *Glory Be*, etc.

Fruit of the Mystery: ***Obedience***

Fifth Joyful Mystery:
The Finding of the Child Jesus in the Temple

On the third day they came upon Him in the temple sitting in the midst of the teachers, listening to them and asking them questions.   (*Luke* 2:46)

One *Our Father*, Ten *Hail Marys*,
One *Glory Be*, etc.

Fruit of the Mystery: ***Joy in Finding Jesus***

First Luminous Mystery:
The Baptism of Jesus

And when Jesus was baptized . . . the heavens were opened and He saw the Spirit of God descending like a dove, and alighting on Him, and lo, a voice from heaven, saying "this is My beloved Son," with whom I am well pleased."   (*Matthew* 3:16-17)

One *Our Father*, Ten *Hail Marys*,
One *Glory Be*, etc.

Fruit of the Mystery: ***Openness to the Holy Spirit***

Second Luminous Mystery:
The Wedding at Cana

His mother said to the servants, "Do whatever He tells you." . . . Jesus said to them, "Fill the jars with water." And they filled them up to the brim.

(John 2:5-7)

One *Our Father*, Ten *Hail Marys*,
One *Glory Be*, etc.

Fruit of the Mystery: ***To Jesus through Mary***

Third Luminous Mystery:
The Proclamation of God's Kingdom

"And preach as you go, saying, 'The kingdom of heaven is at hand.' Heal the sick, raise the dead, cleanse lepers, cast out demons. You received without pay, give without pay."

(Matthew 10:7-8)

One *Our Father*, Ten *Hail Marys*,
One *Glory Be*, etc.

Fruit of the Mystery: ***Repentance and Trust in God***

Fourth Luminous Mystery:
The Transfiguration

And as He was praying, the appearance of His countenance was altered and His raiment become dazzling white. And a voice came out of the cloud saying, "This is My Son, My chosen; listen to Him!

(Luke 9:29, 35)

One *Our Father*, Ten *Hail Marys*,
One *Glory Be*, etc.

Fruit of the Mystery: ***Desire for Holiness***

Fifth Luminous Mystery:
The Institution of the Eucharist

And He took bread, and when He had given thanks He broke it and gave it to them, saying, "This is My body which is given for you." . . . And likewise the cup after supper, saying, "This cup which is poured out for you is the new covenant in My blood."
(Luke 22:19-20)
One *Our Father*, Ten *Hail Marys*,
One *Glory Be*, etc.
Fruit of the Mystery: *Adoration*

First Sorrowful Mystery:
The Agony in the Garden

In His anguish He prayed with all the greater intensity, and His sweat became like drops of blood falling to the ground. Then He rose from prayer and came to His disciples, only to find them asleep, exhausted with grief. (*Luke* 22:44-45)
One *Our Father*, Ten *Hail Marys*,
One *Glory Be*, etc.
Fruit of the Mystery: *Sorrow for Sin*

Second Sorrowful Mystery:
The Scourging at the Pillar

Pilate's next move was to take Jesus and have Him scourged.
(*John* 19:1)
One *Our Father*, Ten *Hail Marys*,
One *Glory Be*, etc.
Fruit of the Mystery: *Purity*

Third Sorrowful Mystery:
The Crowning with Thorns

They stripped off His clothes and wrapped Him in a scarlet military cloak. Weaving a crown out of thorns they fixed it on His head, and stuck a reed in His right hand . . . (Matthew 27:28-29)
One *Our Father*, Ten *Hail Marys*,
One *Glory Be*, etc.
Fruit of the Mystery: *Courage*

Fourth Sorrowful Mystery:
The Carrying of the Cross

. . . carrying the cross by Himself, He went out to what is called the Place of the Skull (in Hebrew, Golgotha).   (*John* 19:17)

One *Our Father*, Ten *Hail Marys*,
One *Glory Be*, etc.

Fruit of the Mystery: **Patience**

Fifth Sorrowful Mystery:
The Crucifixion

Jesus uttered a loud cry and said, "Father, into Your hands I commend My spirit." After He said this, He expired.   (*Luke* 23:46)

One *Our Father*, Ten *Hail Marys*,
One *Glory Be*, etc.

Fruit of the Mystery: **Perseverance**

First Glorious Mystery:
The Resurrection

You need not be amazed! You are looking for Jesus of Nazareth, the one who was crucified. He has been raised up; He is not here. See the place where they laid Him."   (*Mark* 16:6)

One *Our Father*, Ten *Hail Marys*,
One *Glory Be*, etc.

Fruit of the Mystery: **Faith**

Second Glorious Mystery:
The Ascension

Then, after speaking to them, the Lord Jesus was taken up into Heaven and took His seat at God's right hand.   (*Mark* 16:19)

One *Our Father*, Ten *Hail Marys*,
One *Glory Be*, etc.

Fruit of the Mystery: **Hope**

Third Glorious Mystery:
The Descent of the Holy Spirit

All were filled with the Holy Spirit. They began to express themselves in foreign tongues and make bold proclamation as the
Spirit prompted them.   (*Acts* 2:4)

One *Our Father*, Ten *Hail Marys*,
One *Glory Be*, etc.

Fruit of the Mystery: ***Love of God***

Fourth Glorious Mystery:
The Assumption

You are the glory of Jerusalem . . . you are the splendid boast of
our people . . . God is pleased with what you have wrought. May
you be blessed by the Lord Almighty forever and ever.

(*Judith* 15:9-10)

One *Our Father*, Ten *Hail Marys*,
One *Glory Be*, etc.

Fruit of the Mystery: ***Grace of a Happy Death***

Fifth Glorious Mystery:
The Coronation

A great sign appeared in the sky, a woman clothed with the sun,
with the moon under her feet, and on her head a crown of twelve
stars.   (*Revelation* 12:1)

One *Our Father*, Ten *Hail Marys*,
One *Glory Be*, etc.

Fruit of the Mystery: ***Trust in Mary's Intercession***

The Volumes

Direction for Our Times
as given to Anne, a lay apostle

Volume One: *Thoughts on Spirituality*
Volume Two: *Conversations with the*
Eucharistic Heart of Jesus
Volume Three: *God the Father Speaks to*
His Children
The Blessed Mother Speaks
to Her Bishops and Priests
Volume Four: *Jesus The King*
Heaven Speaks to Priests
Jesus Speaks to Sinners
Volume Six: *Heaven Speaks to Families*
Volume Seven: *Greetings from Heaven*
Volume Nine: *Angels*
Volume Ten: *Jesus Speaks to His Apostles*

Volumes 5 and 8 will be printed at a later date.

These books are available at
www.directionforourtimes.com
or at your local bookstore.

The *Heaven Speaks* Booklets
Direction for Our Times
as given to Anne, a lay apostle

These booklet are from the series *Direction for Our Times as given to Anne, a lay apostle.* They are available individually from Direction for Our Times and are listed below:

Heaven Speaks About Abortion
Heaven Speaks About Addictions
Heaven Speaks to Victims of Clerical Abuse
Heaven Speaks to Consecrated Souls
Heaven Speaks About Depression
Heaven Speaks About Divorce
Heaven Speaks to Prisoners
Heaven Speaks to Soldiers
Heaven Speaks About Stress
Heaven Speaks to Young Adults

New in 2007:

Heaven Speaks to Those Away from the Church
Heaven Speaks to Those Considering Suicide
Heaven Speaks to Those Who Are Dying
Heaven Speaks to Those Who Do Not Know Jesus
Heaven Speaks to Those Who Experience Tragedy
Heaven Speaks to Those Who Fear Purgatory
Heaven Speaks to Those Who Have Rejected God
Heaven Speaks to Those Who Struggle to Forgive
Heaven Speaks to Those Who Suffer from Financial Need
Heaven Speaks to Parents Who Worry About
  Their Children's Salvation

Other Written Works by Anne, a lay apostle

The Mist of Mercy

Anne begins this full-length book by telling us that the enemy of God is present on earth and a battle is being waged for souls. Satan is trying to destroy God's plan for us, which is unity with Him in heaven for eternity. We must be alert to these efforts and be armed for the battle. This is the reality of spiritual warfare.

Following is a section entitled *Snapshots of Reality* which is a collection of short stories depicting realistic earthly struggles while including a glimpse of these same situations from the heavenly perspective and how our friends, the saints, act on our behalf more than we can imagine.

Also in this book is Anne's account of her mystical experiences of purgatory. She tells us of the souls she saw there and describes the prayers they prayed and the remorse they felt for the choices they had made on earth which were against the will of God. You will be happy to learn that purgatory is a great mercy of God and allows each soul there the perfect experience of preparation for eternity in heaven.

The last section is a reprint of the Monthly Messages from Jesus Christ dated from December 1, 2004 through June 1, 2006.

In Defense of Obedience
and
Reflections on the Priesthood

This newly published work by Anne consists of two essays on topics close to the heart of Jesus. The first is entitled *In Defense of Obedience* and the second is entitled *Reflections on the Priesthood*.

In Defense of Obedience is a serious call to return to a spirit of obedience to the Magisterium of the Church. Obedience to the Church is a must for every apostle, laity and clergy alike.

Anne's essay on the priesthood gives us the smallest glimpse of the love Our Lord has for the men who hear and answer His call. We read the depth of the connection Jesus has with these men and how they are united in a most unique way to the Sacred Heart of Jesus and the Immaculate Heart of Mary. This is also a gentle reminder that we are called to love and support our priests who serve us in their humanity but with a heavenly dignity bestowed upon them from heaven by Jesus Christ, the First Priest.

Interviews with Anne, a lay apostle

VHS tapes and DVDs featuring Anne, a lay apostle, have been produced by Focus Worldwide Network and can be purchased by visiting our website at:

www.directionforourtimes.com

Focus Worldwide Television Network

Char Vance works on a team with the Focus Worldwide Television Network in New Orleans, Louisiana. Focus is owned and operated by Retired Archbishop Philip Hannan. Focus Worldwide Television Network produces high quality Catholic programming.

Char Vance

Nora McCarthy with Archbishop Hannan

This book is part of a non-profit mission.
Our Lord has requested that we
spread these words internationally.

Please help us.

If you would like to assist us financially,
please send your tax-deductible contribution
to the address below:

Direction for Our Times
9000 West 81st Street
Justice, Illinois 60458

www.directionforourtimes.com

Email: contactus@directionforourtimes.com
Phone: 708-496-9300

Direction For Our Times—Ireland
Lisnalea
Virginia Rd.
Bailieborough
Co. Cavan.
Republic of Ireland

www.directionforourtimes.com

Email: dfotireland@yahoo.ie
Phone: 353-(0)42-969-4947

Direction for Our Times is a 501(c)(3)
not-for-profit corporation. Contributions are
deductible to the extent provided by law.

Jesus gives Anne a message for the world on
the first of each month. To receive the
monthly messages you may access our
website at www.directionforourtimes.com
or call us at 708-496-9300
to be placed on our mailing list.